CROCK·POT®
◆ THE ORIGINAL SLOW COOKER ◆

5 INGREDIENTS or LESS

Publications International, Ltd.

Pictured on the front cover: French Onion Soup *(page 134)*.

Pictured on the back cover *(left to right):* Hot Beef Sandwiches au Jus *(page 60)*, Blueberry-Banana Pancakes *(page 30)* and Shredded Pork Wraps *(page 82)*.

ISBN: 978-1-68022-297-5

Library of Congress Control Number: 2015935363

Manufactured in China.

8 7 6 5 4 3 2 1

Publications International, Ltd.

TABLE OF CONTENTS

SLOW COOKING TIPS

Sizes of CROCK-POT® Slow Cookers

Smaller **CROCK-POT®** slow cookers—such as 1- to 3½-quart models—are the perfect size for cooking for singles, a couple or empty nesters (and also for serving dips).

While medium-size **CROCK-POT®** slow cookers (those holding somewhere between 3 quarts and 5 quarts) will easily cook enough food at a time to feed a small family. They are also convenient for holiday side dishes or appetizers.

Large **CROCK-POT®** slow cookers are great for large family dinners, holiday entertaining and potluck suppers. A 6- to 7-quart model is ideal if you like to make meals in advance, or have dinner tonight and store leftovers for another day.

Types of CROCK-POT® Slow Cookers

Current **CROCK-POT®** slow cookers come equipped with many different features and benefits, from auto cook programs to oven-safe stoneware to timed programming. Please visit **WWW.CROCK-POT.COM** to find the **CROCK-POT®** slow cooker that best suits your needs.

How you plan to use a **CROCK-POT®** slow cooker may affect the model you choose to purchase. For everyday cooking, choose a size large enough to serve your family. If you plan to use the **CROCK-POT®** slow cooker primarily for entertaining, choose one of the larger sizes. Basic **CROCK-POT®** slow cookers can hold as little as 16 ounces or as much as 7 quarts. The smallest sizes are great for keeping dips warm on a buffet, while the larger sizes can more readily fit large quantities of food and larger roasts.

Cooking, Stirring and Food Safety

CROCK-POT® slow cookers are safe to leave unattended. The outer heating base may get hot as it cooks, but it should not pose a fire hazard. The heating element in the heating base functions at a low wattage and is safe for your countertops.

Your **CROCK-POT®** slow cooker should be filled about one-half to three-fourths full for most recipes unless otherwise instructed. Lean meats such as chicken or pork tenderloin will cook faster than meats with more connective tissue and fat such as beef chuck or pork shoulder. Bone-in meats will take longer than boneless cuts. Typical **CROCK-POT®** slow cooker dishes take approximately 7 to 8 hours to reach the simmer point on LOW and about 3 to 4 hours on HIGH. Once the vegetables and meat start to simmer and braise, their flavors will fully blend and meat will become fall-off-the-bone tender.

According to the U.S. Department of Agriculture, all bacteria are killed at a temperature of 165°F. It's important to follow the recommended cooking times and not to open the lid often, especially early in the cooking process when heat is building up inside the unit. If you need to open the lid to check on your food or are adding additional ingredients, remember to allow additional cooking time if necessary to ensure food is cooked through and tender.

Large **CROCK-POT®** slow cookers, the 6- to 7-quart sizes, may benefit from a quick stir halfway through cook time to help distribute heat and promote even cooking. It's usually unnecessary to stir at all, as even ½ cup liquid will help to distribute heat and the stoneware is the perfect medium for holding food at an even temperature throughout the cooking process.

Oven-Safe Stoneware

All **CROCK-POT®** slow cooker removable stoneware inserts may (without their lids) be used safely in ovens at up to 400°F. In addition, all **CROCK-POT®** slow cookers are microwavable without their lids. If you own another slow cooker brand, please refer to your owner's manual for specific stoneware cooking medium tolerances.

Frozen Food

Frozen food can be successfully cooked in a **CROCK-POT®** slow cooker. However, it will require longer cooking time than the same recipe made with fresh food. It is almost always preferable to thaw frozen food prior to placing it in the **CROCK-POT®** slow cooker. Using an instant-read thermometer is recommended to ensure meat is fully cooked through.

Pasta and Rice

If you are converting a recipe for a **CROCK-POT®** slow cooker that calls for uncooked pasta, first cook the pasta on the stovetop just until slightly tender. Then add the pasta to the **CROCK-POT®** slow cooker. If you are converting a recipe for the **CROCK-POT®** slow cooker that calls for cooked rice, stir in raw rice with the other recipe ingredients plus ¼ cup extra liquid per ¼ cup of raw rice.

Beans

Beans must be softened completely before combining with sugar and/or acidic foods in the **CROCK-POT®** slow cooker. Sugar and acid have a hardening effect on beans and will prevent softening. Fully cooked canned beans may be used as a substitute for dried beans.

Vegetables

Root vegetables often cook more slowly than meat. Cut vegetables accordingly to cook at the same rate as meat—large or small or lean versus marbled—and place near the sides or bottom of the stoneware to facilitate cooking.

Herbs

Fresh herbs add flavor and color when added at the end of the cooking cycle; if added at the beginning, many fresh herbs' flavor will dissipate over long cook times. Ground and/or dried herbs and spices work well in slow cooking and may be added at the beginning of cook time. For dishes with shorter cook times, hearty fresh herbs such as rosemary and thyme hold up well. The flavor power of all herbs and spices can vary greatly depending on their particular strength and shelf life. Use chili powders and garlic powder sparingly, as these can sometimes intensify over the long cook times. Always taste the finished dish and correct seasonings including salt and pepper.

page 84

Liquids

It's not necessary to use more than ½ to 1 cup liquid in most instances since juices in meats and vegetables are retained more in slow cooking than in conventional cooking. Excess liquid can be cooked down and concentrated after slow cooking on the stovetop or by removing meat and vegetables from stoneware, stirring in one of the following thickeners and setting the **CROCK-POT®** slow cooker to HIGH. Cover; cook on HIGH for approximately 15 minutes or until juices are thickened.

FLOUR: All-purpose flour is often used to thicken soups or stews. Stir cold water into the flour in a small bowl until smooth. With the heat on on HIGH, whisk the flour mixture into the liquid in the **CROCK-POT®** slow cooker. Cover; cook on HIGH 15 minutes or until mixture is thickened.

page 138

CORNSTARCH: Cornstarch gives sauces a clear, shiny appearance; it's used most often for sweet dessert sauces and stir-fry sauces. Stir cold water into the cornstarch in a small bowl until the cornstarch dissolves. Quickly stir this mixture into the liquid in the **CROCK-POT®** slow cooker; the sauce will thicken as soon as the liquid simmers. Cornstarch breaks down with too much heat, so never add it at the beginning of the slow

cooking process and turn off the heat as soon as the sauce thickens.

ARROWROOT: Arrowroot (or arrowroot flour) comes from the root of a tropical plant that is dried and ground to a powder; it produces a thick, clear sauce. Those who are allergic to wheat often use it in place of flour. Place arrowroot in a small bowl or cup and stir in cold water until the mixture is smooth. Quickly stir this mixture into the liquid in the **CROCK-POT®** slow cooker. Arrowroot thickens below the boiling point, so it even works well in a **CROCK-POT®** slow cooker on LOW. Too much stirring can break down an arrowroot mixture.

TAPIOCA: Tapioca is a starchy substance extracted from the root of the cassava plant. Its greatest advantage is that it withstands long cooking, making it an ideal choice for slow cooking. Add it at the beginning of cooking and you'll get a clear, thickened sauce in the finished dish. Dishes using tapioca as a thickener are best cooked on the LOW setting; tapioca may become stringy when boiled for a long time.

Milk

Milk, cream and sour cream break down during extended cooking. When possible, add them during the last 15 to 30 minutes of slow cooking, until just heated through. Condensed soups may be substituted for milk and may cook for extended times.

page 108

Fish

Fish is delicate and should be stirred into the **CROCK-POT®** slow cooker gently during the last 15 to 30 minutes of cooking time. Cover; cook just until cooked through and serve immediately.

Baked Goods

If you wish to prepare bread, cakes or pudding cakes in a **CROCK-POT®** slow cooker, you may want to purchase a covered, vented metal cake pan accessory for your **CROCK-POT®** slow cooker. You can also use any straight-sided soufflé dish or deep cake pan that will fit into the stoneware of your unit. Baked goods can be prepared directly in the stoneware; however, they can be a little difficult to remove from the insert, so follow the recipe directions carefully.

page 20

CROCK-POT® Slow Cooker Recipes with 5 Ingredients or Less

A well-stocked pantry is a shortcut to preparing dishes and entire meals efficiently. The five chapters in this cookbook take full advantage of the kinds of everyday ingredients most cooks commonly have on hand. They feature recipes that can be created with 5 ingredients and/or the addition of these common pantry items:

• Water	• Other common spices	• All-purpose flour
• Milk	*(such as ground cinnamon,*	• Cornstarch
• Butter	*ground nutmeg, ground red*	• Arrowroot
	pepper, red pepper flakes,	
• Vegetable oil	*garlic powder, ground cumin,*	• Tapioca
• Olive oil	*ground oregano, dried thyme,*	• Granulated sugar
	chili powder, paprika, etc.)	
• Salt and black pepper		

These slow-cooked recipes are perfect for busy days when you don't have time to make another stop at the grocery store.

MORNING TREATS

Maple, Bacon and Raspberry Pancake

Makes 8 servings

5 slices bacon

2 cups pancake mix

1 cup water

½ cup maple syrup, plus additional for serving

1 cup fresh raspberries

3 tablespoons chopped pecans, toasted*

*To toast pecans, spread in a single layer in heavy skillet. Cook over medium heat 1 to 2 minutes or until nuts are lightly browned, stirring frequently.

1. Heat large skillet over medium heat. Add bacon; cook 7 to 8 minutes or until crisp. Remove to paper-towel lined plate; crumble.

2. Brush inside of 4- to 5-quart oval **CROCK-POT®** slow cooker with 1 to 2 tablespoons bacon fat from skillet. Combine pancake mix, water and ½ cup syrup in large bowl; stir to blend. Pour half of batter into **CROCK-POT®** slow cooker; top with half of raspberries, half of bacon and half of pecans. Pour remaining half of batter over top; sprinkle with remaining raspberries, bacon and pecans.

3. Cover; cook on HIGH 1½ to 2 hours or until pancake has risen and is cooked through. Turn off heat. Let stand, uncovered, 10 to 15 minutes. Remove pancake from **CROCK-POT®** slow cooker; cut into eight pieces. Serve with additional syrup.

Hot Mulled Cider

Makes 16 servings

½ gallon apple cider

½ cup packed brown sugar

1½ teaspoons balsamic or cider vinegar (optional)

1 teaspoon vanilla

1 whole cinnamon stick

6 whole cloves

1. Combine cider, brown sugar, vinegar, if desired, vanilla, cinnamon stick and cloves in **CROCK-POT®** slow cooker. Cover; cook on LOW 5 to 6 hours.

2. Remove and discard cinnamon stick and cloves. Serve warm in mugs.

Whoa Breakfast

Makes 6 servings

3 cups water

2 cups chopped peeled apples

1½ cups steel-cut or old-fashioned oats

¼ cup sliced almonds

½ teaspoon ground cinnamon

Combine water, apples, oats, almonds and cinnamon in **CROCK-POT®** slow cooker. Cover; cook on LOW 8 hours.

Hot Mulled Cider

Banana Nut Bread

Makes 1 loaf

⅓ cup butter

3 mashed bananas

⅔ cup sugar

2 eggs, beaten

2 tablespoons dark corn syrup

1¾ cups all-purpose flour

2 teaspoons baking powder

½ teaspoon salt

¼ teaspoon baking soda

½ cup chopped walnuts

1. Grease and flour inside of **CROCK-POT®** slow cooker. Beat butter in large bowl with electric mixer at medium speed until fluffy. Gradually beat in bananas, sugar, eggs and corn syrup until smooth.

2. Combine flour, baking powder, salt and baking soda in small bowl; stir to blend. Beat flour mixture into banana mixture. Add walnuts; mix thoroughly. Pour batter into **CROCK-POT®** slow cooker.

3. Cover; cook on HIGH 2 to 3 hours. Cool completely; turn bread out onto large serving platter.

Tip: Banana Nut Bread has always been a favorite way to use up those overripe bananas. Not only is it delicious, but it also freezes well for future use.

Banana Nut Bread

Oatmeal with Maple-Glazed Apples and Cranberries

Makes 4 servings

3 cups water

2 cups quick-cooking or old-fashioned oats

¼ teaspoon salt

1 teaspoon unsalted butter

2 medium red or Golden Delicious apples, unpeeled and cut into ½-inch pieces

¼ teaspoon ground cinnamon

2 tablespoons maple syrup

4 tablespoons dried cranberries

1. Combine water, oats and salt in **CROCK-POT®** slow cooker. Cover; cook on LOW 8 hours.

2. Melt butter in large nonstick skillet over medium heat. Add apples and cinnamon; cook and stir 4 to 5 minutes or until tender. Stir in syrup; heat through.

3. Serve oatmeal with apple mixture and dried cranberries.

Tip: For a quick, make-ahead breakfast, freeze this oatmeal in individual portions. It can be reheated quickly in the microwave, saving the fuss of measuring, cooking and cleaning up.

Oatmeal with Maple-Glazed Apples and Cranberries

Cinnamon-Ginger Poached Pears

Makes 6 servings

3 cups water

1 cup sugar

10 slices fresh ginger

2 whole cinnamon sticks

1 tablespoon chopped candied ginger (optional)

6 Bosc or Anjou pears, peeled and cored

1. Combine water, sugar, ginger, cinnamon and candied ginger, if desired, in **CROCK-POT®** slow cooker. Add pears. Cover; cook on LOW 4 to 6 hours or on HIGH 1½ to 2 hours.

2. Remove pears with slotted spoon. Cook syrup, uncovered, on HIGH 30 minutes or until thickened. Remove and discard cinnamon sticks.

Mucho Mocha Cocoa

Makes 9 servings

4 cups whole milk

4 cups half-and-half

1 cup chocolate syrup

⅓ cup instant coffee granules

2 tablespoons sugar

2 whole cinnamon sticks

1. Combine milk, half-and-half, chocolate syrup, coffee granules, sugar and cinnamon sticks in **CROCK-POT®** slow cooker; stir to blend. Cover; cook on LOW 3 hours.

2. Remove and discard cinnamon sticks. Serve warm in mugs.

Cinnamon-Ginger Poached Pears

Orange Date Nut Bread

Makes 10 servings

2 cups all-purpose flour, plus additional for dusting

½ cup chopped pecans

1 teaspoon baking powder

½ teaspoon baking soda

¼ teaspoon salt

1 cup chopped dates

2 teaspoons orange peel

⅔ cup boiling water

¾ cup sugar

2 tablespoons shortening

1 egg, lightly beaten

1 teaspoon vanilla

1. Spray 1-quart soufflé dish, casserole or other high-sided baking dish with nonstick cooking spray; dust with flour.

2. Combine 2 cups flour, pecans, baking powder, baking soda and salt in medium bowl.

3. Combine dates and orange peel in separate medium bowl; pour boiling water over date mixture. Add sugar, shortening, egg and vanilla; stir just until blended.

4. Add flour mixture to date mixture; stir just until blended. Pour batter into prepared dish; place in 4½-quart **CROCK-POT®** slow cooker. Cover; cook on HIGH 2½ hours or until edge begins to brown.

5. Remove dish from **CROCK-POT®** slow cooker. Cool on wire rack 10 minutes. Remove bread from dish; cool completely on wire rack.

Variation: Substitute 1 cup dried cranberries for dates.

Orange Date Nut Bread

Apple and Granola Breakfast Cobbler

Makes 4 servings

4 Granny Smith apples, peeled, cored and sliced

½ cup packed light brown sugar

1 tablespoon lemon juice

1 teaspoon ground cinnamon

2 cups granola cereal, plus additional for garnish

2 tablespoons butter, cut into small pieces

Whipping cream, half-and-half or vanilla yogurt (optional)

1. Place apples in **CROCK-POT®** slow cooker. Sprinkle brown sugar, lemon juice and cinnamon over apples. Stir in 2 cups granola and butter.

2. Cover; cook on LOW 6 hours or on HIGH 2 to 3 hours. Serve warm with additional granola sprinkled on top. Serve with cream, if desired.

Spiced Citrus Tea

Makes 6 servings

4 tea bags

Peel of 1 orange

4 cups boiling water

2 cans (6 ounces *each*) orange-pineapple juice

3 tablespoons honey

3 whole cinnamon sticks

3 star anise

1. Place tea bags, orange peel and boiling water in **CROCK-POT®** slow cooker; cover and let steep 10 minutes. Remove and discard tea bags and orange peel. Add juice, honey, cinnamon sticks and star anise.

2. Cover; cook on LOW 3 hours. Remove and discard cinnamon sticks and star anise.

Apple and Granola Breakfast Cobbler

Breakfast Quinoa

Makes 6 servings

1½ cups uncooked quinoa

3 cups water

3 tablespoons packed brown sugar

2 tablespoons maple syrup

1½ teaspoons ground cinnamon

¾ cup golden raisins

Fresh raspberries and banana slices

1. Place quinoa in fine-mesh strainer; rinse well under cold running water. Remove to **CROCK-POT®** slow cooker.

2. Stir water, brown sugar, maple syrup and cinnamon into **CROCK-POT®** slow cooker. Cover; cook on LOW 5 hours or on HIGH 2½ hours or until quinoa is tender and water is absorbed.

3. Add raisins during last 10 to 15 minutes of cooking time. Top quinoa with raspberries and bananas.

Breakfast Quinoa

Zucchini Bread

Makes 1 loaf

1⅔ cups all-purpose flour, plus additional for dusting

1¼ teaspoons ground cinnamon

1 teaspoon baking powder

½ teaspoon salt

½ teaspoon ground allspice

¼ teaspoon baking soda

1 cup sugar

2 eggs, lightly beaten

½ cup canola oil

1 tablespoon vanilla

1 large zucchini, trimmed and shredded

½ cup chopped walnuts

1. Spray inside of 8½×4½×2¾-inch ovenproof glass or ceramic loaf pan* that fits inside **CROCK-POT®** slow cooker with nonstick cooking spray; dust with flour.

2. Combine 1⅔ cups flour, cinnamon, baking powder, salt, allspice and baking soda in medium bowl; stir to blend. Whisk sugar, eggs, oil and vanilla in another medium bowl. Pour sugar mixture into flour mixture; stir until just moistened. Gently fold in zucchini and walnuts. Pour into prepared loaf pan. Place in **CROCK-POT®** slow cooker. Cover; cook on HIGH 3½ to 3¾ hours or until toothpick inserted into center comes out clean.

3. Remove bread from **CROCK-POT®** slow cooker; let cool in pan 10 minutes. Remove bread from pan; let cool on wire rack 30 minutes before slicing.

*You may also use a glass bowl that fits inside of the **CROCK-POT®** slow cooker.*

Viennese Coffee

Makes 4 servings

3 cups strong freshly brewed hot coffee

3 tablespoons chocolate syrup

1 teaspoon sugar

⅓ cup whipping cream, plus additional for topping

¼ cup crème de cacao or Irish cream

Chocolate shavings (optional)

1. Combine coffee, chocolate syrup and sugar in **CROCK-POT®** slow cooker. Cover; cook on LOW 2 to 2½ hours.

2. Stir ⅓ cup whipping cream and crème de cacao into **CROCK-POT®** slow cooker. Cover; cook on LOW 30 minutes or until heated through. Ladle coffee into coffee cups. Top with additional whipped cream and chocolate shavings, if desired.

Bacon and Cheese Brunch Potatoes

Makes 6 servings

3 medium russet potatoes (about 2 pounds), peeled and cut into 1-inch cubes

1 cup chopped onion

½ teaspoon seasoned salt

4 slices bacon, crisp-cooked and crumbled

1 cup (4 ounces) shredded sharp Cheddar cheese

1 tablespoon water

1. Coat inside of **CROCK-POT®** slow cooker with nonstick cooking spray. Place half of potatoes in **CROCK-POT®** slow cooker. Sprinkle half of onion and seasoned salt over potatoes; top with half of bacon and cheese. Repeat layers. Sprinkle water over top.

2. Cover; cook on LOW 6 hours or on HIGH 3½ hours or until potatoes and onion are tender. Stir gently to mix; serve warm.

Viennese Coffee

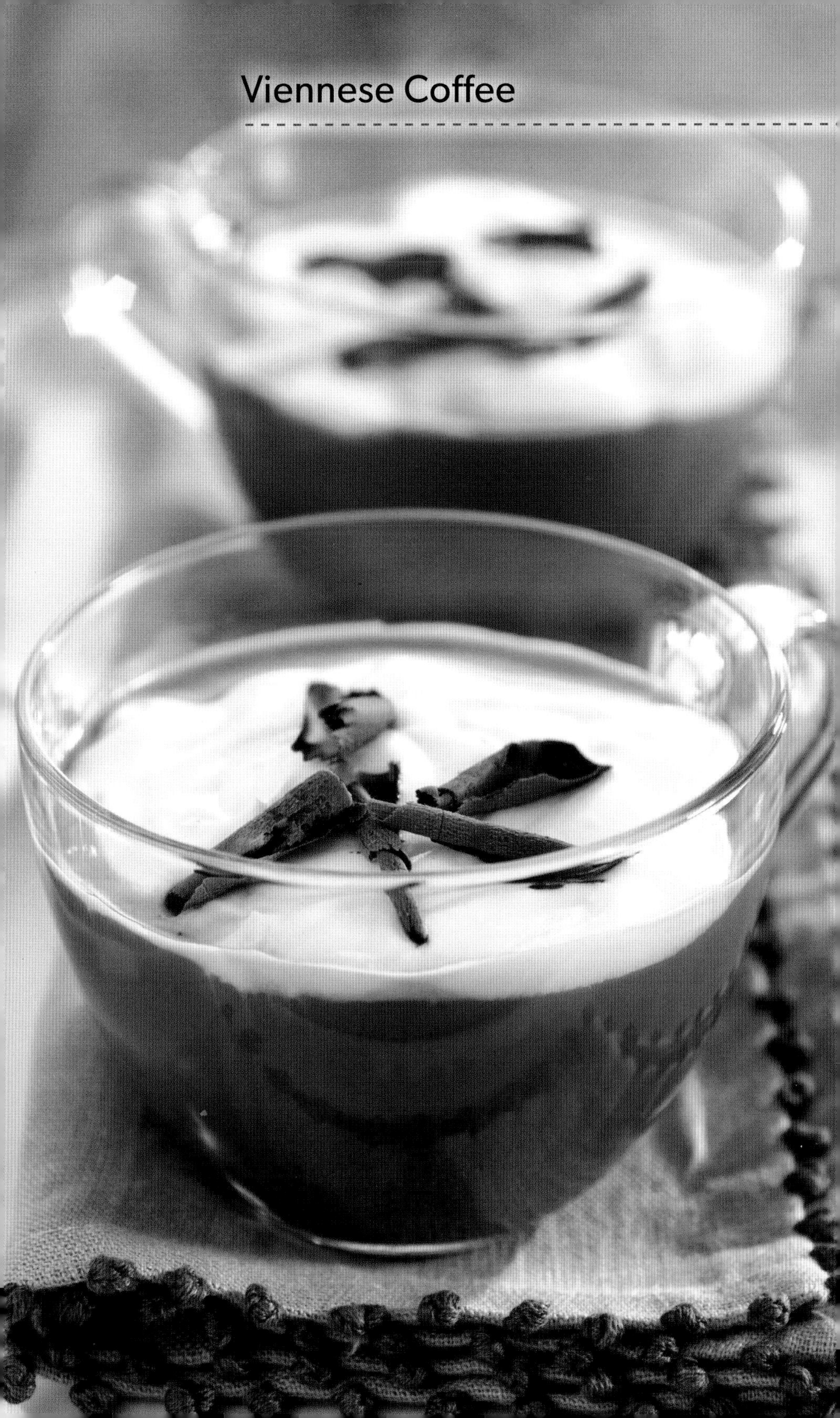

Blueberry-Banana Pancakes

Makes 8 servings

2 cups all-purpose flour

⅓ cup sugar

1 tablespoon baking powder

½ teaspoon baking soda

½ teaspoon salt

½ teaspoon ground cinnamon

1¾ cups milk

2 eggs, lightly beaten

¼ cup (½ stick) unsalted butter, melted

1 teaspoon vanilla

1 cup fresh blueberries

2 small bananas, sliced (optional)

Maple syrup (optional)

1. Combine flour, sugar, baking powder, baking soda, salt and cinnamon in medium bowl; stir to blend. Combine milk, eggs, butter and vanilla in separate medium bowl; stir to blend. Pour milk mixture into flour mixture; stir until moistened. Gently fold in blueberries until combined.

2. Coat inside of **CROCK-POT®** slow cooker with nonstick cooking spray. Remove batter to **CROCK-POT®** slow cooker. Cover; cook on HIGH 2 hours or until puffed and toothpick inserted into center comes out clean. Cut into wedges; top with bananas and maple syrup, if desired.

Blueberry-Banana Pancakes

Cinnamon Latté

Makes 6 to 8 servings

6 cups double-strength brewed coffee*

2 cups half-and-half

1 cup sugar

1 teaspoon vanilla

3 whole cinnamon sticks, plus additional for garnish

Whipped cream (optional)

*Double the amount of coffee grounds normally used to brew coffee. Or substitute 8 teaspoons instant coffee dissolved in 6 cups boiling water.

1. Blend coffee, half-and-half, sugar and vanilla in 3- to 4-quart **CROCK-POT®** slow cooker. Add 3 cinnamon sticks. Cover; cook on HIGH 3 hours.

2. Remove and discard cinnamon sticks. Serve latté in tall coffee mugs. Garnish with additional cinnamon sticks and whipped cream.

Tip: Cinnamon sticks are useful for flavoring hot beverages such as cinnamon latté, hot chocolate, coffee, tea and mulled wine. (Do not add ground cinnamon to simmering or boiling liquids, because it will clump and cause a gritty texture, and the cinnamon will lose its flavor.)

Cinnamon Latté

Spiced Vanilla Applesauce

Makes 6 cups

5 pounds (about 10 medium) sweet apples (such as Fuji or Gala), peeled and cut into 1-inch pieces

½ cup water

2 teaspoons vanilla

1 teaspoon ground cinnamon

¼ teaspoon ground nutmeg

¼ teaspoon ground cloves

1. Combine apples, water, vanilla, cinnamon, nutmeg and cloves; stir to blend. Cover; cook on HIGH 3 to 4 hours or until apples are very tender.

2. Turn off heat. Mash mixture with potato masher to smooth out any large lumps. Let cool completely before serving.

Cinnamon Roll-Topped Mixed Berry Cobbler

Makes 8 servings

2 bags (12 ounces *each*) frozen mixed berries, thawed

1 cup sugar

¼ cup quick-cooking tapioca

¼ cup water

2 teaspoons vanilla

1 package (about 12 ounces) refrigerated cinnamon rolls with icing

Combine berries, sugar, tapioca, water and vanilla in **CROCK-POT®** slow cooker; top with cinnamon rolls. Cover; cook on LOW 4 to 5 hours. Serve warm, drizzled with icing.

Note: This recipe was designed to work best in a 4-quart **CROCK-POT®** slow cooker. Double the ingredients for larger **CROCK-POT®** slow cookers, but always place cinnamon rolls in a single layer.

Spiced Vanilla Applesauce

ASIAN FLAVORS

Hoisin Sriracha Chicken Wings

Makes 5 to 6 servings

3 pounds chicken wings, tips removed and split at joints

½ cup hoisin sauce, divided

¼ cup plus 1 tablespoon sriracha sauce, divided

2 tablespoons packed brown sugar

Sliced green onions (optional)

1. Coat inside of **CROCK-POT®** slow cooker with nonstick cooking spray. Preheat broiler. Spray large baking sheet with nonstick cooking spray. Arrange wings on prepared baking sheet. Broil 6 to 8 minutes or until browned, turning once. Remove wings to **CROCK-POT®** slow cooker.

2. Combine hoisin sauce, ¼ cup sriracha sauce and brown sugar in medium bowl; stir to blend. Pour sauce mixture over wings in **CROCK-POT®** slow cooker; stir to coat. Cover; cook on LOW 3½ to 4 hours. Remove wings to large serving platter; cover with foil to keep warm.

3. Turn **CROCK-POT®** slow cooker to HIGH. Cook, uncovered, on HIGH 10 to 15 minutes or until sauce is thickened. Stir in remaining 1 tablespoon sriracha sauce. Spoon sauce over wings to serve. Garnish with green onions.

Steamed Pork Buns

Makes 16 servings

½ (18-ounce) container refrigerated cooked shredded pork in barbecue sauce*

1 tablespoon Asian garlic chili sauce

1 package (about 16 ounces) refrigerated big biscuit dough (8 biscuits)

Dipping Sauce (recipe follows)

Sliced green onions (optional)

Look for pork in plain, not smoky, barbecue sauce. Substitute chicken in barbecue sauce, if desired.

1. Combine pork and chili sauce in medium bowl; stir to blend. Split biscuits in half. Roll or stretch each biscuit into 4-inch circle. Spoon 1 tablespoon pork onto center of each biscuit. Gather edges around filling and press to seal.

2. Generously butter 2-quart baking dish that fits inside 5- to 6-quart **CROCK-POT®** slow cooker. Arrange filled biscuits in single layer, overlapping slightly if necessary. Cover dish with buttered foil, butter side down.

3. Place small rack in **CROCK-POT®** slow cooker. Add 1 inch of hot water (water should not touch top of rack). Place baking dish on rack. Cover; cook on HIGH 2 hours.

4. Meanwhile, prepare Dipping Sauce. Garnish pork buns with green onions and serve with Dipping Sauce.

Dipping Sauce: Stir together 2 tablespoons rice vinegar, 2 tablespoons soy sauce, 4 teaspoons sugar and 1 teaspoon toasted sesame oil in a small bowl until sugar dissolves. Sprinkle with 1 tablespoon minced green onion just before serving.

Tip: Straight-sided round casserole or soufflé dishes that fit inside the **CROCK-POT®** stoneware make excellent baking dishes.

Steamed Pork Buns

Vietnamese Chicken Pho

Makes 4 to 6 servings

8 cups chicken broth

2 to 3 cups shredded cooked chicken

8 ounces bean sprouts

Rice stick noodles

1 bunch Thai basil, chopped

Hoisin sauce (optional)

Lime wedges (optional)

1. Combine broth and chicken in **CROCK-POT®** slow cooker. Cover; cook on LOW 6 to 7 hours or on HIGH 3 hours.

2. Add bean sprouts, noodles and Thai basil. Cover; cook on HIGH 20 minutes or until noodles are softened.

3. Spoon soup into individual serving bowls. Serve with hoisin sauce and lime wedges, if desired.

Note: A simple soup to prepare with leftover shredded chicken, this classic Asian chicken noodle soup packs tons of flavor.

Vietnamese Chicken Pho

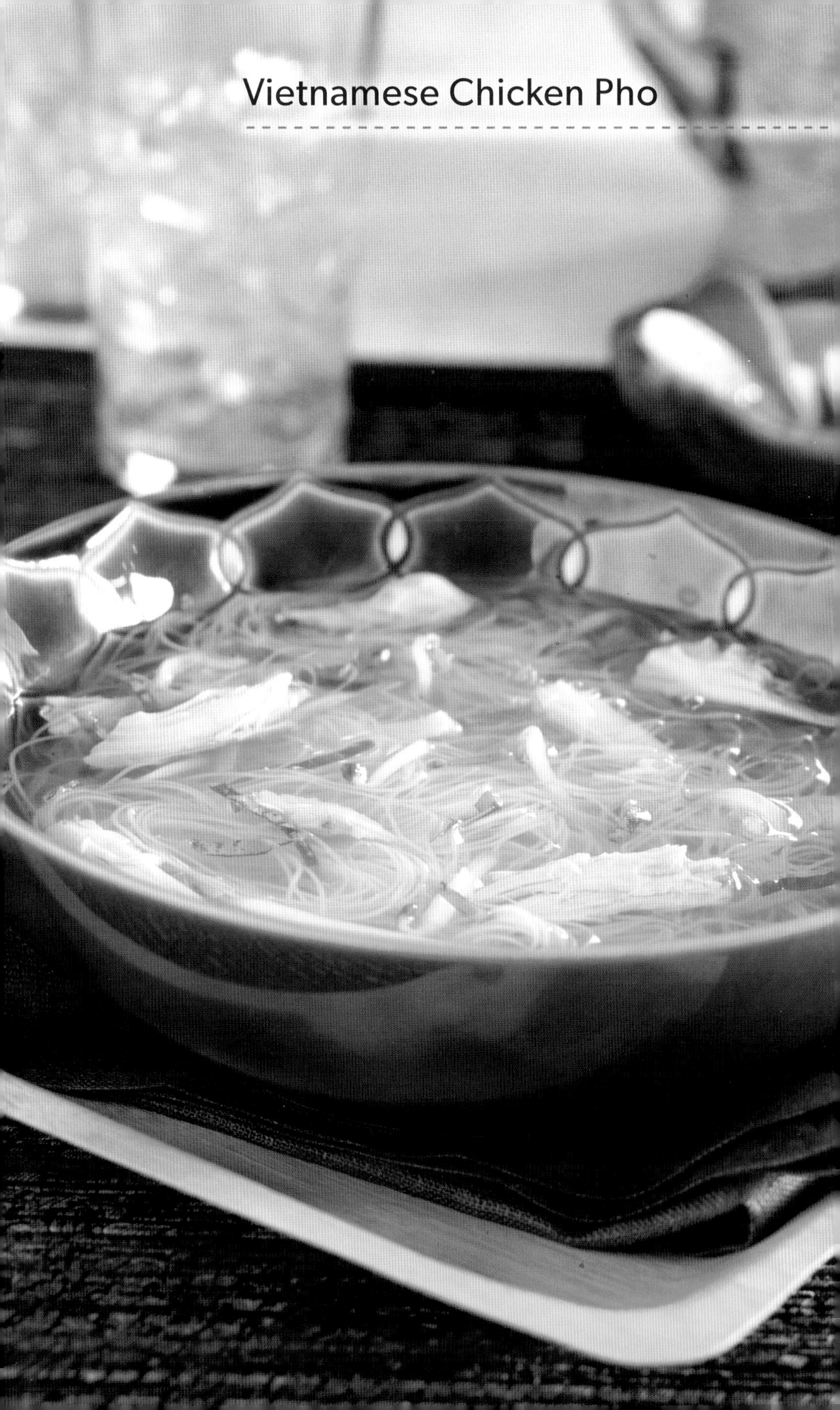

Asian Beef with Broccoli

Makes 4 to 6 servings

1½ pounds boneless beef chuck roast (about 1½ inches thick), sliced into thin strips*

1 can (10½ ounces) condensed beef broth, undiluted

½ cup oyster sauce

2 tablespoons cornstarch

1 bag (16 ounces) fresh broccoli florets

Hot cooked rice

Sesame seeds (optional)

Freeze steak 30 minutes to make slicing easier.

1. Place beef in **CROCK-POT®** slow cooker. Pour broth and oyster sauce over beef. Cover; cook on HIGH 3 hours.

2. Stir 2 tablespoons cooking liquid into cornstarch in small bowl until smooth; whisk into cooking liquid. Cover; cook on HIGH 15 minutes or until thickened.

3. Cook broccoli according to package directions. Add to **CROCK-POT®** slow cooker; toss gently. Serve with rice; garnish with sesame seeds.

Asian Beef with Broccoli

Thai Chicken Wings

Makes 8 to 10 servings

1 tablespoon peanut oil

5 pounds chicken wings, tips removed and split at joints

½ cup unsweetened canned coconut milk

1 tablespoon sugar

1 tablespoon Thai green curry paste

1 tablespoon fish sauce

¾ cup prepared spicy peanut sauce

Sliced green onions (optional)

1. Heat oil in large skillet over medium-high heat. Add wings in batches; cook 3 to 5 minutes or until browned on all sides. Remove to **CROCK-POT®** slow cooker using slotted spoon.

2. Stir coconut milk, sugar, curry paste and fish sauce into **CROCK-POT®** slow cooker. Cover; cook on LOW 6 to 7 hours or on HIGH 3 to 3½ hours. Remove wings with slotted spoon to large bowl; toss with peanut sauce before serving. Garnish with green onions.

Thai Chicken Wings

Best Asian-Style Ribs

Makes 6 to 8 servings

2 full racks pork baby back ribs, split into 3 sections *each*

6 ounces hoisin sauce

½ cup maraschino cherries, drained

½ cup rice wine vinegar

2 tablespoons minced fresh ginger

Combine ribs, hoisin sauce, cherries, vinegar and ginger in **CROCK-POT**® slow cooker. Cover; cook on LOW 6 to 7 hours or on HIGH 3 to 3½ hours.

Tip: Baby back pork ribs are called "baby" because they are smaller than spareribs. They're cut from the loin of the pig, cook in less time and are more tender than spareribs.

Best Asian-Style Ribs

Curried Lentils with Fruit

Makes 6 servings

5 cups water

1½ cups dried brown lentils, rinsed and sorted

1 Granny Smith apple, chopped, plus additional for garnish

¼ cup golden raisins

¼ cup lemon yogurt

1 teaspoon salt

1 teaspoon curry powder

1. Combine water, lentils, 1 chopped apple and raisins in **CROCK-POT®** slow cooker; stir to blend. Cover; cook on LOW 8 to 9 hours or until most liquid is absorbed.

2. Remove lentil mixture to large bowl; stir in yogurt, salt and curry powder until blended. Garnish with additional apple.

Curried Lentils with Fruit

Spicy Orange Chicken Nuggets

Makes 8 to 9 servings

1 bag (28 ounces) frozen popcorn chicken bites

1½ cups prepared honey teriyaki marinade

¾ cup orange juice concentrate

⅔ cup water

1 tablespoon orange marmalade

½ teaspoon hot chile sauce or sriracha*

Hot cooked rice with peas and corn

Sriracha is a Thai hot sauce and is available in Asian specialty markets and large supermarkets.

1. Preheat oven to 450°F. Spread chicken evenly on baking sheet. Bake 12 to 14 minutes or until crisp. (Do not brown.) Remove to **CROCK-POT®** slow cooker.

2. Combine teriyaki marinade, juice concentrate, water, marmalade and chile sauce in medium bowl; stir to blend. Pour over chicken. Cover; cook on LOW 3 to 3½ hours. Serve with rice.

Spicy Orange Chicken Nuggets

Spicy Asian Pork Bundles

Makes 20 bundles

1 boneless pork sirloin roast (about 3 pounds)*

½ cup soy sauce

1 tablespoon chili garlic sauce or chili paste

2 teaspoons minced fresh ginger

2 tablespoons water

1 tablespoon cornstarch

2 teaspoons dark sesame oil

1 cup shredded carrots

10 large lettuce leaves

*Unless you have a 5-, 6- or 7-quart **CROCK-POT®** slow cooker, cut any roast larger than 2½ pounds in half so it cooks completely.*

1. Combine pork, soy sauce, chili garlic sauce and ginger in **CROCK-POT®** slow cooker; mix well. Cover; cook on LOW 8 to 10 hours.

2. Remove roast to large cutting board; shred with two forks. Let cooking liquid stand 5 minutes to allow fat to rise. Skim off and discard fat.

3. Stir water, cornstarch and oil in small bowl until smooth; whisk into cooking liquid. Turn **CROCK-POT®** slow cooker to HIGH. Cook, uncovered, on HIGH 10 minutes or until sauce is thickened.

4. Stir in shredded pork and carrots. Cover; cook on HIGH 15 to 30 minutes or until heated through. Place ¼ cup pork filling into lettuce leaves. Wrap to enclose.

Mu Shu Pork Bundles: Lightly spread prepared plum sauce over small warm flour tortillas. Spoon ¼ cup pork filling and ¼ cup stir-fried vegetables into flour tortillas. Wrap to enclose. Serve immediately. Makes about 20 wraps.

Spicy Asian Pork Bundles

Asian Ginger Chicken Wings

Makes 6 to 8 servings

3 pounds chicken wings, tips removed and split at joints

1 cup chopped red onion

1 cup soy sauce

¾ cup packed brown sugar

¼ cup dry sherry

2 tablespoons chopped fresh ginger

2 cloves garlic, minced

Chopped fresh chives

1. Preheat broiler. Broil chicken about 5 minutes per side. Remove to **CROCK-POT®** slow cooker.

2. Combine onion, soy sauce, brown sugar, sherry, ginger and garlic in medium bowl; stir to blend. Add to **CROCK-POT®** slow cooker; stir to coat. Cover; cook on LOW 5 to 6 hours or on HIGH 2 to 3 hours. Sprinkle with chives.

Tip: You can also leave the wings whole and place them directly into the **CROCK-POT®** slow cooker. Removal of the tips and separating the double-boned piece from the drummette is optional.

Asian Ginger Chicken Wings

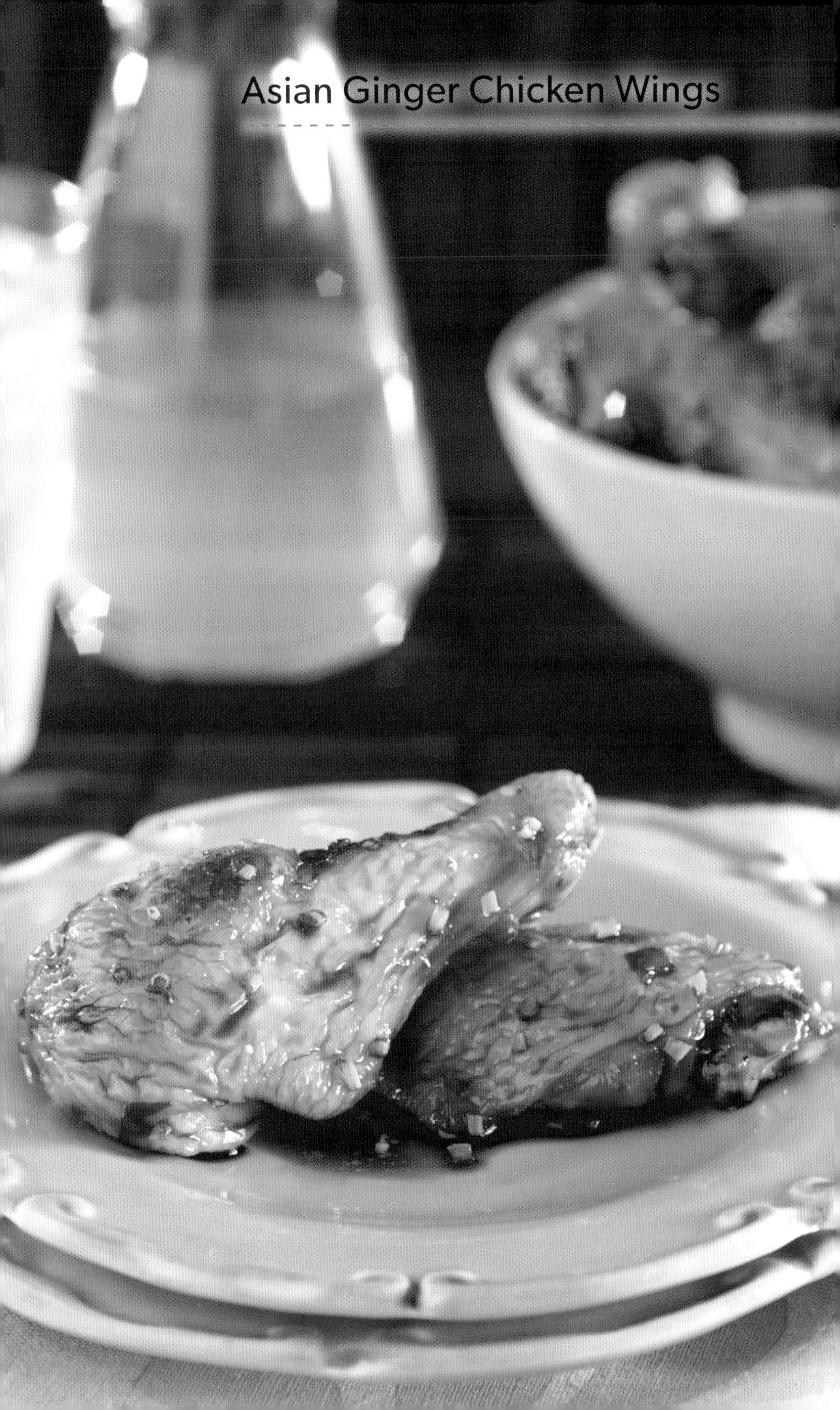

Curried Butternut Squash Soup

Makes 8 servings

2 pounds butternut squash, rinsed, peeled, cored and chopped into 1-inch cubes

1 apple, peeled, cored and chopped

1 medium onion, chopped

5 cups chicken broth

1 tablespoon curry powder

¼ teaspoon ground cloves

Salt and black pepper

¼ cup chopped dried cranberries (optional)

1. Place squash, apple and onion in **CROCK-POT®** slow cooker.

2. Combine broth, curry powder and cloves in small bowl; stir to blend. Pour mixture into **CROCK-POT®** slow cooker. Cover; cook on LOW 5 to 5½ hours or on HIGH 4 hours.

3. Place soup in batches in food processor or blender; process to desired consistency. Season with salt and pepper. Garnish with cranberries.

Curried Butternut Squash Soup

Hot and Sour Chicken

Makes 4 to 6 servings

4 to 6 boneless, skinless chicken breasts (1 to 1½ pounds total)

1 cup chicken broth

1 package (about 1 ounce) dry hot-and-sour soup mix

Sugar snap peas and chopped red bell pepper (optional)

Place chicken in **CROCK-POT®** slow cooker; add broth and dry soup mix. Cover; cook on LOW 5 to 6 hours. Serve over peas and bell peppers, if desired.

Tip: Here are a few simple steps to follow if you decide to debone your own chicken breasts.

1. For easier handling, freeze the chicken until it is firm, but not hard. Then remove the skin.

2. For each breast half, use a sharp knife to make three or four arched cuts between the meat and the bone, lifting the meat away with your free hand. (Or, slip your fingers between the meat and the bone. Then work the meat free without the aid of a knife.)

3. When the meat and bone are separated, remove the heavy white tendon that runs along the length of the breast. This will prevent the meat from shrinking as it cooks.

ASIAN FLAVORS

Hot and Sour Chicken

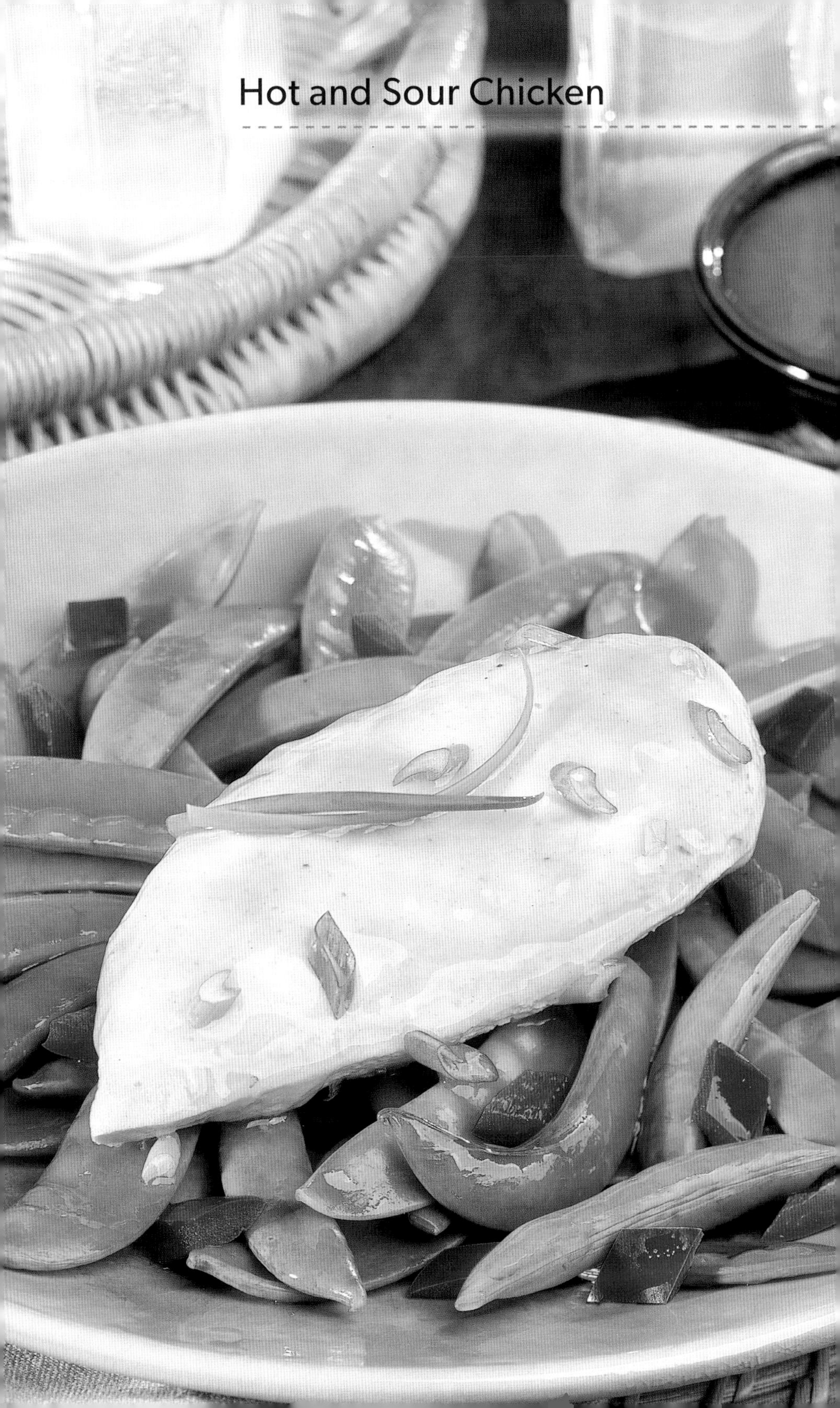

ROASTIN' AROUND

Hot Beef Sandwiches au Jus

Makes 8 to 10 servings

4 pounds boneless beef bottom round roast, trimmed*

2 cans (about 10 ounces *each*) condensed beef broth, undiluted

1 can (12 ounces) beer

2 envelopes (1 ounce *each*) dry onion-flavor soup mix

1 tablespoon minced garlic

2 teaspoons sugar

1 teaspoon dried oregano

Crusty French rolls, sliced in half

*Unless you have a 5-, 6- or 7-quart **CROCK-POT®** slow cooker, cut any roast larger than 2½ pounds in half so it cooks completely.*

1. Place beef in **CROCK-POT®** slow cooker. Combine broth, beer, dry soup mix, garlic, sugar and oregano in large bowl; stir to blend. Pour mixture over beef. Cover; cook on HIGH 6 to 8 hours.

2. Remove beef to large cutting board; shred with two forks. Return beef to cooking liquid; stir to blend. Serve on rolls with cooking liquid for dipping.

Simple Shredded Pork Tacos

Makes 6 servings

2 pounds boneless pork roast

1 cup salsa

1 can (4 ounces) chopped mild green chiles

½ teaspoon garlic salt

½ teaspoon black pepper

Corn or flour tortillas

Optional toppings: salsa, sour cream, jalapeño pepper slices, diced tomatoes, shredded cheese and/or shredded lettuce

1. Place roast, 1 cup salsa, chiles, garlic salt and pepper in **CROCK-POT®** slow cooker. Cover; cook on LOW 8 hours.

2. Remove pork to large cutting board; shred with two forks. Serve on tortillas with sauce and desired toppings.

Tip: To warm tortillas, stack 6 to 8 tortillas and wrap them in plastic wrap. Microwave at HIGH about 40 to 50 seconds, turning over and rotating ¼ turn once during heating. For 1 or 2 tortillas, wrap and heat at HIGH about 20 seconds.

 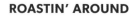

Simple Shredded Pork Tacos

Barbecue Roast Beef

Makes 10 to 12 servings

2 pounds cooked boneless beef roast

1 bottle (12 ounces) barbecue sauce

1½ cups water

10 to 12 sandwich rolls, split

1. Combine beef roast, barbecue sauce and water in **CROCK-POT®** slow cooker. Cover; cook on LOW 2 hours.

2. Remove beef to cutting board; shred with two forks. Return beef to sauce; mix well. Serve on rolls.

Tip: To save time, freeze leftovers as individual portions. Just reheat in a microwave for fast meals!

Barbecue Roast Beef

Rough-Cut Smoky Red Pork Roast

Makes 8 servings

1 boneless pork shoulder roast (about 4 pounds)*

1 can (about 14 ounces) stewed tomatoes, drained

1 can (6 ounces) tomato paste with basil, oregano and garlic

1 cup chopped red bell pepper

2 to 3 canned chipotle peppers in adobo sauce, finely chopped and mashed with fork**

1½ to 2 tablespoons sugar

1 teaspoon salt

*Unless you have a 5-, 6- or 7-quart **CROCK-POT®** slow cooker, cut any roast larger than 2½ pounds in half so it cooks completely.*

**For less heat, remove seeds from chipotle peppers before mashing.*

1. Coat inside of **CROCK-POT®** slow cooker with nonstick cooking spray. Add pork, fat side up. Combine tomatoes, tomato paste, bell pepper and chipotle peppers in small bowl; stir to blend. Pour over pork. Cover; cook on HIGH 5 hours.

2. Scrape tomato mixture into cooking liquid. Remove pork to large cutting board; loosely cover with foil. Let stand 15 minutes before slicing. Stir sugar and salt into cooking liquid. Cook, uncovered, on HIGH 15 minutes or until sauce is thickened. Pour sauce over pork slices to serve.

Rough-Cut Smoky Red Pork Roast

Italian Beef

Makes 8 servings

1 boneless beef rump roast
(3 to 5 pounds)*

1 can (about 14 ounces) beef
broth

2 cups mild giardiniera

8 crusty Italian bread rolls, split

*Unless you have a 5-, 6- or 7-quart **CROCK-POT®**
slow cooker, cut any roast larger than 2½ pounds
in half so it cooks completely.*

1. Place beef in **CROCK-POT®** slow cooker; add broth and giardiniera.
Cover; cook on LOW 10 hours.

2. Remove beef to large cutting board; shred with two forks. Return beef
to cooking liquid; stir to blend. To serve, spoon beef and sauce onto rolls.

Simple Slow Cooker Pork Roast

Makes 6 servings

4 to 5 red potatoes, cut into halves

4 carrots, cut into 1-inch pieces

1 marinated pork loin roast (3 to 4 pounds)*

½ cup water

1 package (10 ounces) frozen baby peas

Salt and black pepper

*If marinated roast is unavailable, combine ¼ cup olive oil, 1 tablespoon minced garlic and 1½ tablespoons Italian seasoning in large resealable food storage bag. Add pork; turn to coat. Marinate in refrigerator at least 2 hours or overnight.

1. Layer potatoes, carrots and pork roast in **CROCK-POT®** slow cooker. (If necessary, cut roast in half to fit.) Add water. Cover; cook on LOW 6 to 8 hours.

2. Add peas during last hour of cooking. Remove pork to large serving platter. Season with salt and pepper. Slice and serve with vegetables.

Dad's Dill Beef Roast

Makes 6 to 8 servings

1 boneless beef chuck roast (3 to 4 pounds)*

1 large jar whole dill pickles, undrained

Unless you have a 5-, 6-, or 7-quart **CROCK-POT® slow cooker, cut any roast larger than 2½ pounds in half so it cooks completely.*

Place beef in **CROCK-POT®** slow cooker. Pour pickles with juice over top of beef. Cover; cook on LOW 8 to 10 hours. Remove beef to large plate; shred with two forks.

Serving Suggestions: Pile this beef onto toasted rolls or buns. Or, for an easy dinner variation, serve it with mashed potatoes.

Simple Slow Cooker
Pork Roast

Easy Family Burritos

Makes 8 servings

1 boneless beef chuck shoulder roast (2 to 3 pounds)*

1 jar (24 ounces) *or* 2 jars (16 ounces *each*) salsa

Flour tortillas, warmed

Optional toppings: shredded cheese, sour cream, salsa, shredded lettuce, diced tomato, diced onion and/or guacamole

*Unless you have a 5-, 6- or 7-quart **CROCK-POT®** slow cooker, cut any roast larger than 2½ pounds in half so it cooks completely.

1. Place beef in **CROCK-POT®** slow cooker; top with salsa. Cover; cook on LOW 8 to 10 hours.

2. Remove beef to large cutting board; shred with two forks. Return to cooking liquid; stir to blend. Cover; cook on LOW 30 minutes or until heated through. Serve in tortillas. Top as desired.

Easy Family Burritos

Fantastic Pot Roast

Makes 6 servings

1 can (12 ounces) cola

1 bottle (10 ounces) chili sauce

2 cloves garlic (optional)

2½ pounds boneless beef chuck roast

Fresh green beans, cooked (optional)

Hot cooked hominy (optional)

Combine cola, chili sauce and garlic, if desired, in **CROCK-POT®** slow cooker. Add beef; turn to coat. Cover; cook on LOW 6 to 8 hours. Serve with cooking liquid, beans and hominy, if desired.

Tip: Chili sauce is closely related to ketchup, but it has a chunkier consistency and a spicy kick. It is based on tomatoes, onions and bell peppers. And has a sweet-and-sour flavor achieved by the balance of sugar and distilled vinegar. The slight heat comes from the use of either chili peppers or chili powder. Although chili sauce is generally considered a condiment, it is sometimes used as an ingredient.

Fantastic Pot Roast

Easy Homemade
Barbecue Sandwiches

Makes 8 servings

1 boneless pork butt roast (3 to 4 pounds)*

Salt and black pepper

1 bottle (16 ounces) barbecue sauce

8 hamburger buns or sandwich rolls, toasted

*Unless you have a 5-, 6- or 7-quart **CROCK-POT®** slow cooker, cut any roast larger than 2½ pounds in half so it cooks completely.*

1. Pour water into bottom of **CROCK-POT®** slow cooker to depth of 1 inch. Season roast with salt and pepper; place in **CROCK-POT®** slow cooker. Cover; cook on LOW 8 to 10 hours.

2. Remove roast to large cutting board. Cover loosely with foil; let stand 10 to 15 minutes. Discard any liquid. Shred roast using two forks.

3. Turn **CROCK-POT®** slow cooker to HIGH. Return meat to **CROCK-POT®** slow cooker. Add barbecue sauce; mix well. Cover; cook on HIGH 30 minutes. Serve barbecue mixture on buns.

Note: Depending on the size of your roast, you may not need to use an entire bottle of barbecue sauce.

Easy Homemade
Barbecue Sandwiches

Best-Ever Roast

Makes 6 to 8 servings

1 can (10¾ ounces) condensed cream of mushroom soup, undiluted

1 package (about 1 ounce) dry onion soup mix

1 boneless beef chuck shoulder roast (3 to 5 pounds)*

4 to 5 medium potatoes, unpeeled and quartered

4 cups baby carrots

*Unless you have a 5-, 6- or 7-quart **CROCK-POT®** *slow cooker, cut any roast larger than 2½ pounds in half so it cooks completely.*

1. Combine mushroom soup and dry soup mix in **CROCK-POT®** slow cooker; stir to blend. Place roast in **CROCK-POT®** slow cooker. Cover; cook on LOW 4 hours.

2. Stir in potatoes and carrots. Cover; cook on LOW 2 hours.

Best-Ever Roast

- -

Peppered Beef Tips

Makes 2 to 3 servings

1 pound boneless beef round tip roast or round steak, cut into 1- to 1½-inch cubes

2 cloves garlic, minced

Black pepper

1 can (10¾ ounces) condensed French onion soup, undiluted

1 can (10¾ ounces) condensed cream of mushroom soup, undiluted

Hot cooked rice or noodles

Place beef in **CROCK-POT®** slow cooker. Season beef with garlic and pepper. Pour soups over beef. Cover; cook on LOW 8 to 10 hours. Serve over rice.

Root Beer BBQ Pulled Pork

Makes 8 servings

1 can (12 ounces) root beer

1 bottle (18 ounces) sweet barbecue sauce, divided

1 package (1 ounce) dry onion soup mix

1 (6- to 8-pound) boneless pork shoulder roast

Salt and black pepper

Hamburger buns

1. Coat inside of **CROCK-POT®** slow cooker with nonstick cooking spray. Combine root beer and ½ bottle barbecue sauce in medium bowl. Rub dry soup mix on pork roast. Place barbecue mixture and roast in **CROCK-POT®** slow cooker. Cover; cook on LOW 8 to 10 hours.

2. Remove pork to large cutting board; shred with two forks. Reserve 1 cup barbecue mixture in **CROCK-POT®** slow cooker; discard remaining mixture. Turn **CROCK-POT®** slow cooker to HIGH. Stir shredded pork, remaining ½ bottle barbecue sauce, salt and pepper into **CROCK-POT®** slow cooker. Cover; cook on HIGH 20 minutes or until heated through. Serve on buns.

Peppered Beef Tips

Shredded Pork Wraps

Makes 6 servings

1 cup salsa, divided

2 tablespoons cornstarch

1 boneless pork sirloin roast
  (2 pounds)

6 (8-inch) flour tortillas

3 cups broccoli slaw mix

½ cup (2 ounces) shredded
  Cheddar cheese

1. Stir ¼ cup salsa into cornstarch in small bowl until smooth. Pour cornstarch mixture into **CROCK-POT®** slow cooker. Top with pork. Pour remaining ¾ cup salsa over pork. Cover; cook on LOW 6 to 8 hours.

2. Remove pork to large cutting board; shred with two forks. Divide shredded meat evenly among tortillas. Spoon about 2 tablespoons salsa mixture on top of meat in each tortilla. Top evenly with broccoli slaw and cheese. Fold bottom edge of tortilla over filling; fold in sides. Roll up completely to enclose filling. Serve remaining salsa mixture as dipping sauce.

Shredded Pork Wraps

So Simple Supper!

Makes 8 servings

1 boneless beef chuck shoulder roast (3 to 4 pounds), trimmed*

3 cups water

1 package (about 1 ounce) dry onion soup mix

1 package (about 1 ounce) au jus gravy mix

1 package (about 1 ounce) mushroom gravy mix

Assorted vegetables (potatoes, carrots, onions and celery)

*Unless you have a 5-, 6- or 7-quart **CROCK-POT®** slow cooker, cut any roast larger than 2½ pounds in half so it cooks completely.*

1. Place beef in **CROCK-POT®** slow cooker. Combine water, dry soup mix and gravy mixes in large bowl; stir to blend. Pour gravy mixture over beef in **CROCK-POT®** slow cooker. Cover; cook on LOW 4 hours.

2. Add vegetables. Cover; cook on LOW 4 hours.

So Simple Supper!

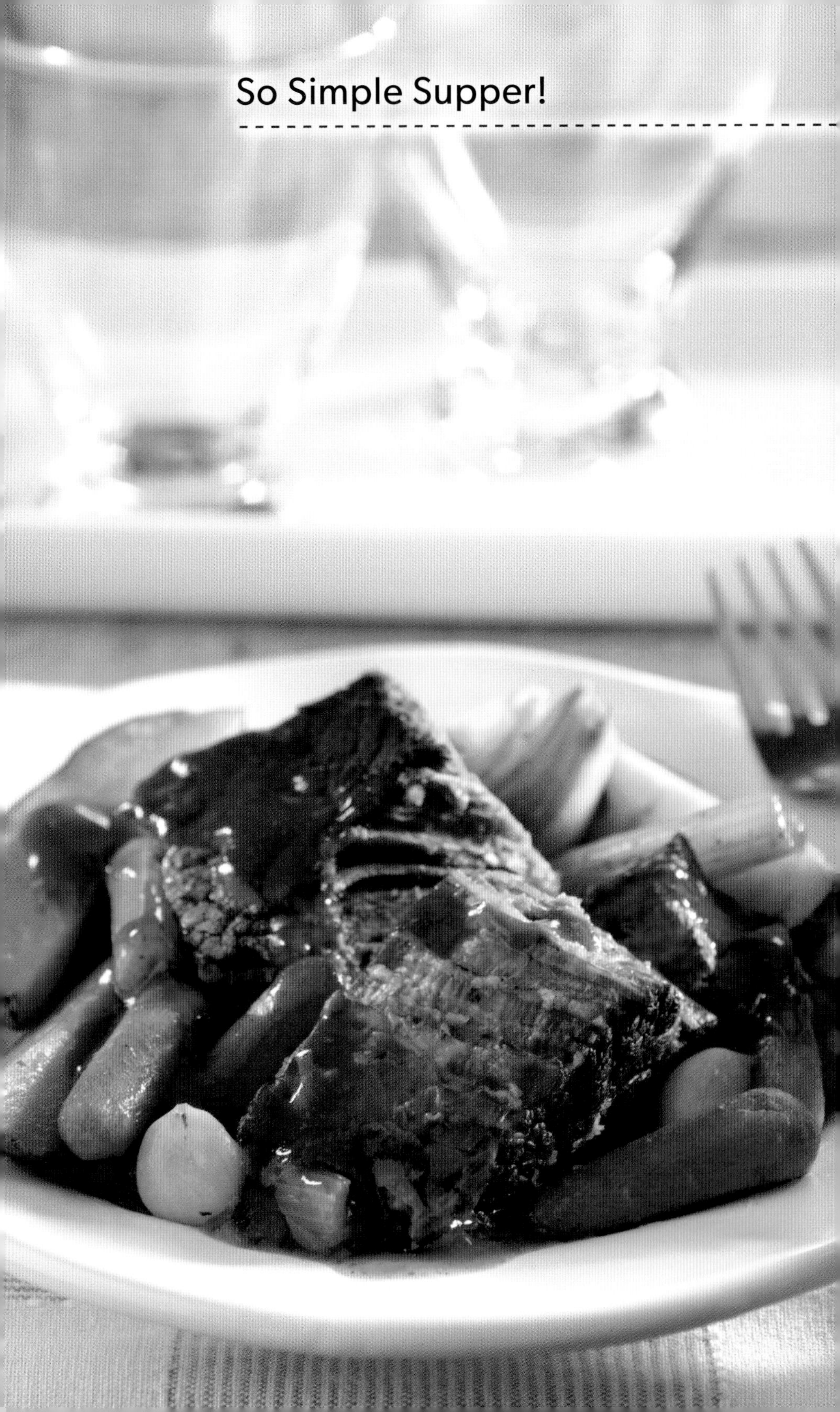

ITALIAN AND MEXICAN

Manchego Eggplant

Makes 12 servings

1 cup all-purpose flour

4 large eggplants, peeled and sliced horizontally into ¾-inch-thick pieces

2 tablespoons olive oil

1 jar (24 to 26 ounces) roasted garlic-flavor pasta sauce

2 tablespoons Italian seasoning

1 cup (4 ounces) grated manchego cheese

1 jar (24 to 26 ounces) roasted eggplant-flavor marinara pasta sauce

1. Place flour in medium shallow bowl. Add eggplant; toss to coat. Heat oil in large skillet over medium-high heat. Lightly brown eggplant in batches 3 to 4 minutes on each side.

2. Pour thin layer of garlic pasta sauce into bottom of **CROCK-POT®** slow cooker. Top with half of eggplant slices, Italian seasoning, cheese and marinara sauce. Repeat layers with remaining half of eggplant slices, Italian seasoning, cheese and marinara sauce. Cover; cook on HIGH 2 hours.

Shredded Beef Wraps

Makes 4 servings

1 beef flank steak or beef skirt steak (1 to 1½ pounds)

1 cup beef broth

½ cup sun-dried tomatoes (not packed in oil), chopped

3 to 4 cloves garlic, minced

¼ teaspoon ground cumin

4 (8-inch) flour tortillas

Shredded lettuce, diced tomatoes and shredded Monterey Jack cheese (optional)

1. Cut flank steak into quarters. Place flank steak, broth, sun-dried tomatoes, garlic and cumin in **CROCK-POT®** slow cooker. Cover; cook on LOW 7 to 8 hours.

2. Remove steak to large cutting board; shred with two forks. Place remaining juices from **CROCK-POT®** slow cooker in blender or food processor; blend until sauce is smooth.

3. Spoon steak onto tortillas with small amount of sauce. Garnish with lettuce, diced tomatoes and cheese.

Creamy Red Pepper Polenta

Makes 4 to 6 servings

6 cups boiling water

2 cups yellow cornmeal

1 small red bell pepper, finely chopped

¼ cup (½ stick) butter, melted

2 teaspoons salt

¼ teaspoon paprika, plus additional for garnish

⅛ teaspoon ground red pepper

⅛ teaspoon ground cumin

Combine water, cornmeal, bell pepper, butter, salt, ¼ teaspoon paprika, ground red pepper and cumin in **CROCK-POT®** slow cooker; stir to blend. Cover; cook on LOW 3 to 4 hours or on HIGH 1 to 2 hours, stirring occasionally. Garnish with additional paprika.

Shredded Beef Wraps

Salsa-Style Wings

Makes 4 servings

2 tablespoons vegetable oil
1½ pounds chicken wings (about 18 wings)

2 cups salsa
¼ cup packed brown sugar
Sprigs fresh cilantro (optional)

1. Heat oil in large skillet over medium-high heat. Add wings in batches; cook 3 to 4 minutes or until browned on all sides. Remove to **CROCK-POT®** slow cooker.

2. Combine salsa and brown sugar in medium bowl; stir to blend. Pour over wings. Cover; cook on LOW 5 to 6 hours or on HIGH 2 to 3 hours. Serve with salsa mixture. Garnish with cilantro.

Cheese Tortellini
with Beef and Mushroom Sauce

Makes 6 servings

½ pound ground beef or turkey
1 jar (24 to 26 ounces) roasted tomato and garlic pasta sauce
1 package (12 ounces) shelf-stable three-cheese tortellini
8 ounces (about 2 cups) sliced button or exotic mushrooms, such as oyster, shiitake or cremini

½ cup water
½ teaspoon red pepper flakes (optional)
¾ cup grated Asiago or Romano cheese

1. Coat inside of **CROCK-POT®** slow cooker with nonstick cooking spray. Brown meat in large skillet over medium heat 6 to 8 minutes, stirring to break up meat. Remove beef to **CROCK-POT®** slow cooker using slotted spoon.

2. Stir in pasta sauce, tortellini, mushrooms, water and red pepper flakes, if desired. Cover; cook on LOW 2 hours or on HIGH 1 hour. Stir.

3. Cover; cook on LOW 2 to 2½ hours or on HIGH ½ to 1 hour. Serve in shallow bowls; top with cheese.

Salsa-Style Wings

Turkey Italian Sausage with White Beans

Makes 4 servings

1 pound turkey or pork Italian sausage, casings removed

½ cup minced onion

2 cans (about 15 ounces *each*) cannellini or Great Northern beans, rinsed and drained

1 can (about 14 ounces) Italian seasoned diced tomatoes

1 teaspoon dried rosemary

½ cup grated Parmesan or Romano cheese

1. Heat large skillet over medium-high heat. Brown sausage and onion 6 to 8 minutes, stirring to break up meat. Drain fat.

2. Coat inside of **CROCK-POT**® slow cooker with nonstick cooking spray. Combine beans, tomatoes and rosemary in **CROCK-POT**® slow cooker. Stir in sausage mixture. Cover; cook on LOW 3 to 4 hours or on HIGH 1½ to 2 hours. Ladle into bowls; top with cheese.

Carne Rellenos

Makes 6 servings

1 can (4 ounces) whole mild green chiles, drained

4 ounces cream cheese, softened

1 flank steak (about 2 pounds)

1½ cups salsa verde

Hot cooked rice (optional)

1. Slit green chiles open on one side with sharp knife; stuff with cream cheese.

2. Open steak flat on sheet of waxed paper. Score steak; turn over. Lay stuffed chiles across unscored side of steak. Roll up; tie with kitchen string.

3. Place steak in **CROCK-POT**® slow cooker; pour in salsa. Cover; cook on LOW 6 to 8 hours or on HIGH 3 to 4 hours. Remove steak to large cutting board. Let stand 10 to 15 minutes before slicing. Serve over rice, if desired, with cooking liquid.

Turkey Italian Sausage with White Beans

Chili Verde

Makes 4 to 8 servings

1 tablespoon vegetable oil

1 to 2 pounds boneless pork chops

2 cups sliced carrots

1 jar (24 ounces) mild green salsa

1 cup chopped onion

1. Heat oil in large skillet over medium-low heat. Add pork; cook 3 to 5 minutes or until browned on both sides.

2. Place carrots in bottom of **CROCK-POT®** slow cooker; top with pork. Pour salsa and onion over pork. Cover; cook on HIGH 6 to 8 hours.

Serving Suggestion: The pork can also be shredded and served in tortillas.

Spicy Shredded Chicken

Makes 6 servings

6 boneless, skinless chicken breasts (about 1½ pounds)

1 jar (16 ounces) salsa

Flour tortillas, warmed

Optional toppings: shredded cheese, sour cream, shredded lettuce, diced tomato, diced onion and/or sliced avocado

1. Place chicken in **CROCK-POT®** slow cooker; top with salsa. Cover; cook on LOW 6 to 8 hours.

2. Remove chicken to large cutting board; shred with two forks. Serve in tortillas. Top as desired.

Chili Verde

Cheesy Polenta

Makes 6 servings

6 cups vegetable broth

1½ cups uncooked medium-grind instant polenta

½ cup grated Parmesan cheese, plus additional for serving

4 tablespoons unsalted butter, cut into cubes

1. Coat inside of **CROCK-POT®** slow cooker with nonstick cooking spray. Heat broth in large saucepan over high heat. Remove to **CROCK-POT®** slow cooker; whisk in polenta.

2. Cover; cook on LOW 2 to 2½ hours or until polenta is tender and creamy. Stir in ½ cup cheese and butter. Serve with additional cheese.

Tip: Spread any leftover polenta in a baking dish and refrigerate until cold. Cut cold polenta into sticks or slices. You can then fry or grill the polenta until lightly browned.

No-Fuss Macaroni and Cheese

Makes 8 servings

2 cups (about 8 ounces) uncooked elbow macaroni

3 ounces pasteurized processed cheese product, cubed

1 cup (4 ounces) shredded mild Cheddar cheese

½ teaspoon salt

⅛ teaspoon black pepper

1½ cups milk

Combine macaroni, cheese product, cheese, salt and pepper in **CROCK-POT®** slow cooker; pour milk over top. Cover; cook on LOW 2 to 3 hours, stirring halfway through cooking time.

Cheesy Polenta

Pesto Rice and Beans

Makes 8 servings

1 can (about 15 ounces) Great Northern beans, rinsed and drained

1 can (about 14 ounces) chicken broth

¾ cup uncooked converted long grain rice

1½ cups frozen cut green beans, thawed and drained

½ cup prepared pesto

Fresh tomato, chopped (optional)

Grated Parmesan cheese (optional)

1. Combine Great Northern beans, broth and rice in **CROCK-POT®** slow cooker; stir to blend. Cover; cook on LOW 2 hours.

2. Stir green beans into **CROCK-POT®** slow cooker. Cover; cook on LOW 1 hour or until rice and beans are tender.

3. Turn off heat. Remove **CROCK-POT®** stoneware to heatproof surface. Stir in pesto. Let stand, covered, 5 minutes. Garnish with tomato and cheese.

Tip: Choose converted long grain rice (or Arborio rice when suggested) or wild rice for best results. Long, slow cooking can turn other types of rice into mush; if you prefer to use another type of rice instead of converted rice, cook it on the stove-top and add it to the **CROCK-POT®** slow cooker during the last 15 minutes of cooking.

Pesto Rice and Beans

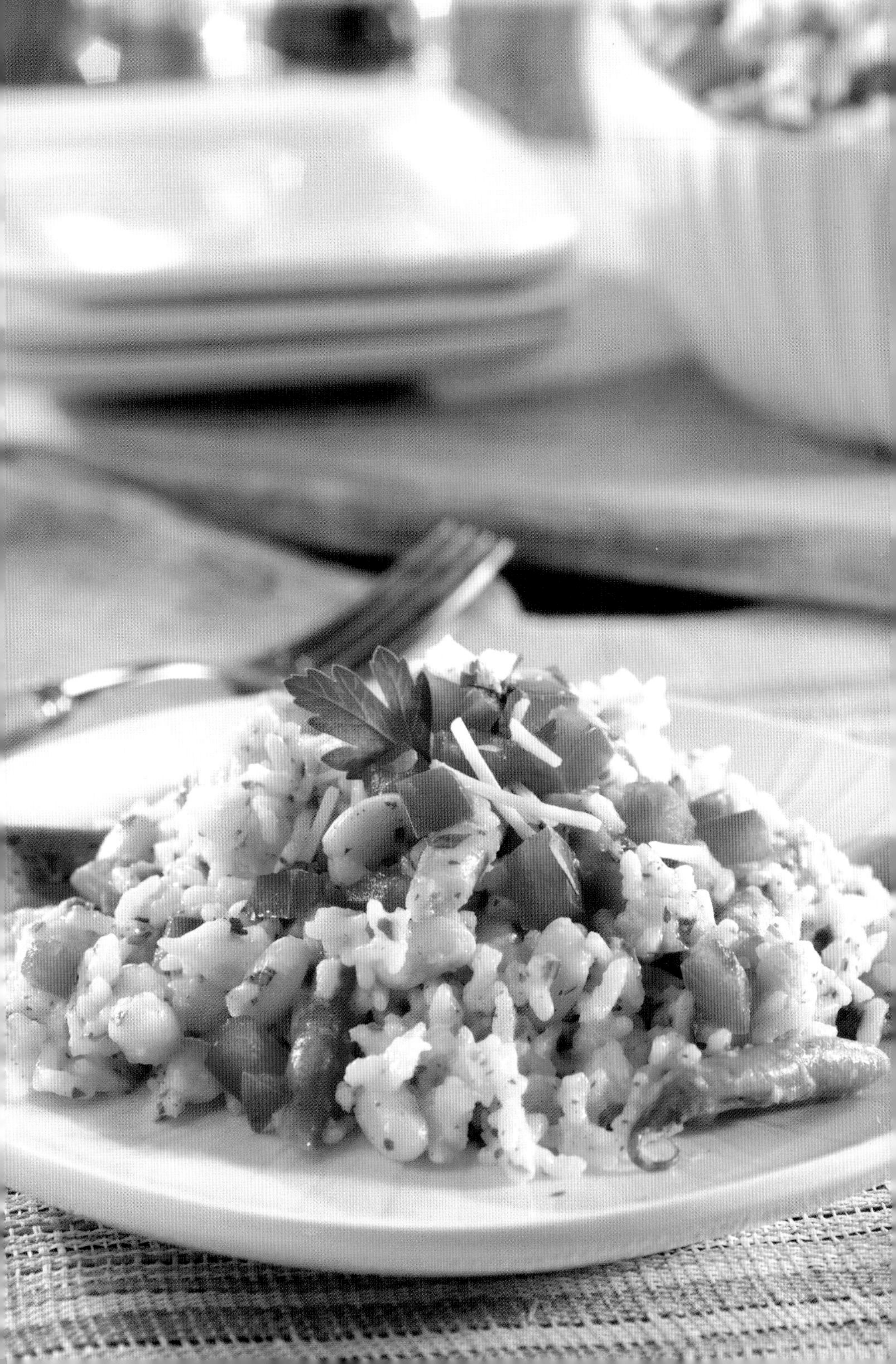

Chicken and Spicy Black Bean Tacos

Makes 4 servings

1 can (about 15 ounces) black beans, rinsed and drained

1 can (10 ounces) diced tomatoes with mild green chiles, drained

1½ teaspoons chili powder

¾ teaspoon ground cumin

1 tablespoon plus 1 teaspoon extra virgin olive oil, divided

12 ounces boneless, skinless chicken breasts

12 crisp corn taco shells

Optional toppings: shredded lettuce, diced tomatoes, shredded Cheddar cheese, sour cream and/or sliced black olives

1. Coat inside of **CROCK-POT**® slow cooker with nonstick cooking spray. Add beans and tomatoes with chiles. Combine chili powder, cumin and 1 teaspoon oil in small bowl; rub onto chicken. Place chicken in **CROCK-POT**® slow cooker. Cover; cook on HIGH 1¾ hours.

2. Remove chicken to large cutting board; slice. Remove bean mixture to large bowl using slotted spoon. Stir in remaining 1 tablespoon oil.

3. To serve, warm taco shells according to package directions. Fill with equal amounts of bean mixture and chicken. Top as desired.

Chicken and Spicy
Black Bean Tacos

Beefy Tortellini

Makes 6 servings

½ pound ground beef or turkey

1 jar (24 to 26 ounces) roasted tomato and garlic pasta sauce

1 package (12 ounces) uncooked three-cheese tortellini

8 ounces sliced button or exotic mushrooms, such as oyster, shiitake and cremini

½ cup water

½ teaspoon red pepper flakes (optional)

¾ cup grated Asiago or Romano cheese

Chopped fresh Italian parsley (optional)

1. Coat inside of **CROCK-POT®** slow cooker with nonstick cooking spray. Brown beef in large skillet over medium-high heat 6 to 8 minutes, stirring to break up meat. Remove to **CROCK-POT®** slow cooker using slotted spoon.

2. Stir in pasta sauce, tortellini, mushrooms, water and red pepper flakes, if desired. Cover; cook on LOW 2 hours or on HIGH 1 hour. Stir.

3. Cover; cook on LOW 2 to 2½ hours or on HIGH ½ to 1 hour. Serve in shallow bowls topped with cheese and parsley, if desired.

Beefy Tortellini

Mexican-Style Spinach

Makes 6 servings

3 packages (10 ounces *each*) frozen chopped spinach, thawed

1 tablespoon canola oil

1 onion, chopped

1 clove garlic, minced

2 Anaheim chiles, roasted, peeled and minced*

3 fresh tomatillos, roasted, husks removed and chopped**

To roast chiles, heat large heavy skillet over medium-high heat. Add chiles; cook and turn until blackened all over. Place chiles in brown paper bag 2 to 5 minutes. Remove chiles from bag; scrape off charred skin. Cut off top and pull out core. Slice lengthwise; scrape off veins and any remaining seeds with a knife.

**To roast tomatillos, heat large heavy skillet over medium heat. Add tomatillos with papery husks; cook 10 minutes or until husks are brown and interior flesh is soft. Remove and discard husks when cool enough to handle.*

1. Place spinach in **CROCK-POT®** slow cooker.

2. Heat oil in large skillet over medium heat. Add onion and garlic; cook and stir 5 minutes or until onion is tender. Add chiles and tomatillos; cook 3 to 4 minutes. Remove onion mixture to **CROCK-POT®** slow cooker. Cover; cook on LOW 4 to 6 hours.

Mexican-Style Spinach

Posole

Makes 8 servings

3 pounds boneless pork, cubed

2 cans (about 15 ounces *each*) white hominy, drained

1 package (10 ounces) frozen white corn, thawed

¾ cup chili sauce

Combine pork, hominy, corn and chili sauce in **CROCK-POT®** slow cooker; stir to blend. Cover; cook on LOW 10 hours or on HIGH 5 hours.

Mile-High Enchilada Pie

Makes 4 to 6 servings

6 (6-inch) corn tortillas

1 jar (12 ounces) salsa

1 can (about 15 ounces) kidney beans, rinsed and drained

1 cup shredded cooked chicken

1 cup (4 ounces) shredded Monterey Jack cheese with jalapeño peppers

Chopped fresh cilantro and sliced red bell pepper (optional)

1. Prepare foil handles by tearing off three 18×2-inch strips heavy foil (or use regular foil folded to double thickness). Crisscross foil strips in spoke design; place in **CROCK-POT®** slow cooker to make lifting tortilla stack easier. Place 1 tortilla on top of foil handles. Top with small amount of salsa, beans, chicken and cheese. Continue layering in order using remaining ingredients, ending with tortilla and cheese. Cover; cook on LOW 6 to 8 hours or on HIGH 3 to 4 hours.

2. Pull pie out by foil handles. Garnish with fresh cilantro and sliced red bell pepper.

Posole

Pasta Shells with Prosciutto

Makes 4 servings

3 cups (8 ounces) uncooked medium shell pasta

1 jar (24 to 26 ounces) vodka pasta sauce

¾ cup water

½ cup whipping cream

2 ounces (½ cup) torn or coarsely chopped thin sliced prosciutto

¼ cup chopped fresh chives

1. Coat inside of **CROCK-POT®** slow cooker with nonstick cooking spray. Combine pasta, pasta sauce and water in **CROCK-POT®** slow cooker. Cover; cook on LOW 2 hours or on HIGH 1 hour.

2. Stir in cream. Cover; cook on LOW 1 to 1½ hours or on HIGH 45 minutes to 1 hour or until pasta is tender.

3. Stir prosciutto into pasta mixture. Spoon into shallow bowls; top with chives.

Parmesan Potato Wedges

Makes 6 servings

2 pounds red potatoes, cut into ½-inch wedges

¼ cup finely chopped onion

1½ teaspoons dried oregano

½ teaspoon salt

¼ teaspoon black pepper

2 tablespoons butter, cubed

¼ cup grated Parmesan cheese

Layer potatoes, onion, oregano, salt and pepper in **CROCK-POT®** slow cooker; dot with butter. Cover; cook on HIGH 4 hours. Remove potatoes to large serving platter; sprinkle with cheese.

Pasta Shells with Prosciutto

Garlic and Herb Polenta

Makes 6 servings

3 tablespoons butter, divided

8 cups water

2 cups yellow cornmeal

2 teaspoons finely minced garlic

2 teaspoons salt

3 tablespoons chopped fresh herbs such as parsley, chives, thyme or chervil (or a combination)

Coat inside of **CROCK-POT®** slow cooker with 1 tablespoon butter. Stir in water, cornmeal, garlic, salt and remaining 2 tablespoons butter. Cover; cook on LOW 4 hours or on HIGH 3 hours, stirring occasionally. Stir in chopped herbs just before serving.

Dulce de Leche

Makes about 1½ cups

1 can (14 ounces) sweetened condensed milk

Pour milk into 9×5-inch loaf pan; cover tightly with foil. Place loaf pan in **CROCK-POT®** slow cooker. Pour enough water to reach halfway up sides of loaf pan. Cover; cook on LOW 5 to 6 hours or until golden and thickened.

Serving Suggestion: Try this Dulce de Leche as a fondue with bananas, apples, shortbread, chocolate wafers, pretzels and/or waffle cookies.

Garlic and Herb Polenta

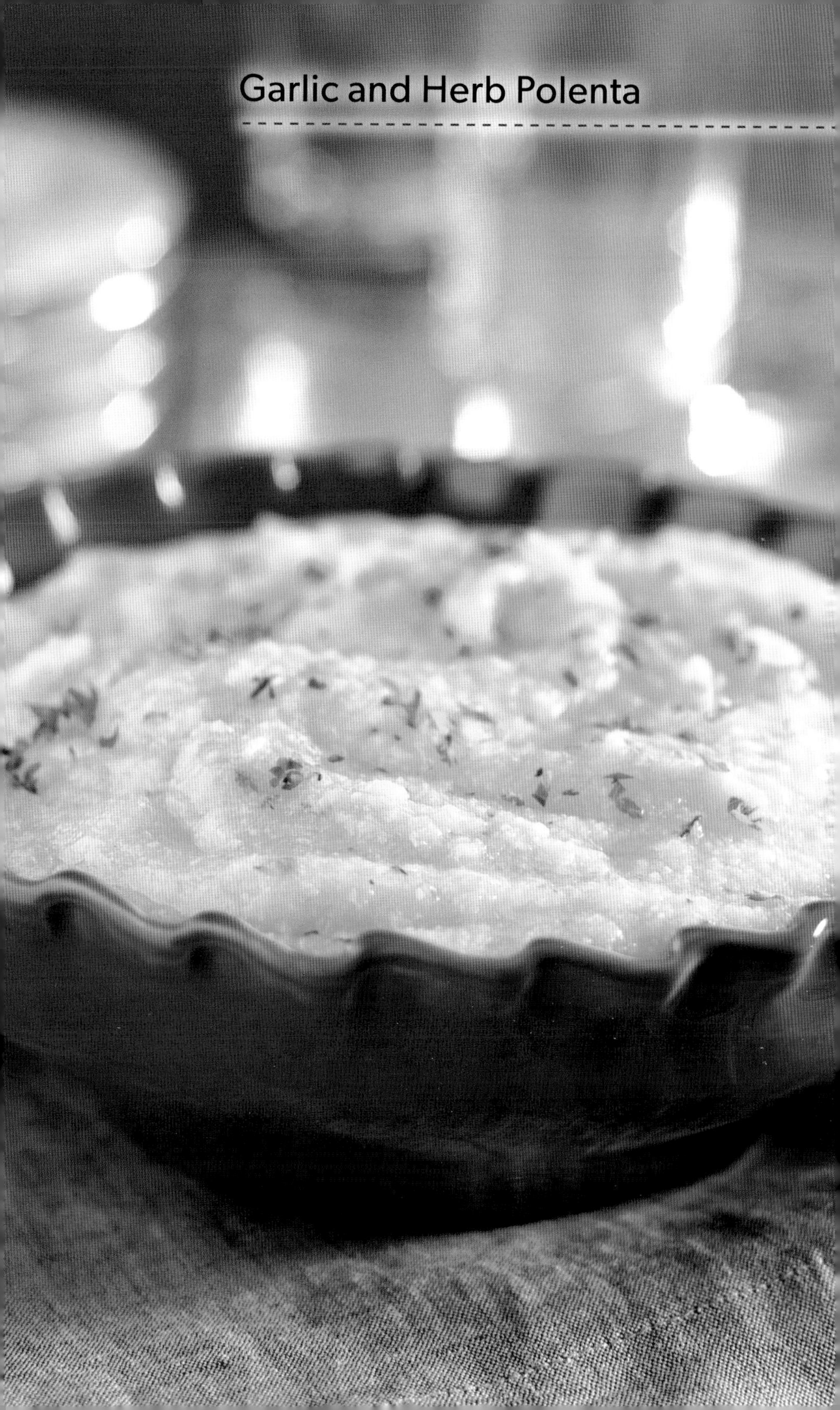

VEGETARIAN FAVORITES

Olive Oil Mashed Rutabagas

Makes 8 servings

1 (2½ to 3-pound) rutabaga (waxed turnip), peeled and cut into 1-inch pieces

4 cloves garlic

Boiling water

2 tablespoons olive oil

1 teaspoon dried thyme

1 teaspoon salt

1. Combine rutabaga, garlic and enough boiling water to cover by 1 inch in **CROCK-POT®** slow cooker. Cover; cook on LOW 7 to 8 hours.

2. Place rutabaga in food processor or blender; purée, adding water as necessary to reach desired consistency. Stir in oil, salt and thyme.

Beans and Spinach Bruschetta

Makes 16 servings

2 cans (about 15 ounces *each*) Great Northern or cannellini beans

3 cloves garlic, minced

Salt and black pepper

3 tablespoons extra virgin olive oil, divided

6 cups spinach, loosely packed and finely chopped

1 tablespoon red wine vinegar

16 slices whole grain baguette

1. Combine beans, garlic, salt and black pepper in **CROCK-POT®** slow cooker; stir to blend. Cover; cook on LOW 3 hours or until beans are tender. Turn off heat. Mash beans with potato masher.

2. Heat 1 tablespoon oil in large skillet over medium heat. Add spinach; cook 2 minutes or until wilted. Stir in vinegar, salt and pepper. Remove from heat.

3. Preheat grill or broiler. Brush baguette slices with remaining 2 tablespoons oil. Grill 5 to 7 minutes or until bread is golden brown and crisp. Top with bean mixture and spinach.

Kale, Olive Oil and Parmesan Soup

Makes 4 to 6 servings

2 tablespoons olive oil

1 small Spanish onion, sliced

3 cloves garlic, minced

Kosher salt and black pepper

8 cups vegetable broth

2 pounds kale, washed and chopped

Grated Parmesan cheese

Extra virgin olive oil (optional)

1. Heat olive oil in large, heavy skillet over medium-high heat. Add onion, garlic, salt and pepper; cook and stir 4 to 5 minutes or until onion begins to soften. Remove onion mixture to **CROCK-POT®** slow cooker; add broth. Cover; cook on LOW 3 hours or until heated through.

2. Stir in kale. Turn **CROCK-POT®** slow cooker to HIGH. Cover; cook on HIGH 15 minutes or until heated through. Sprinkle each serving with cheese and drizzle with extra virgin olive oil just before serving.

VEGETARIAN FAVORITES

Beans and Spinach Bruschetta

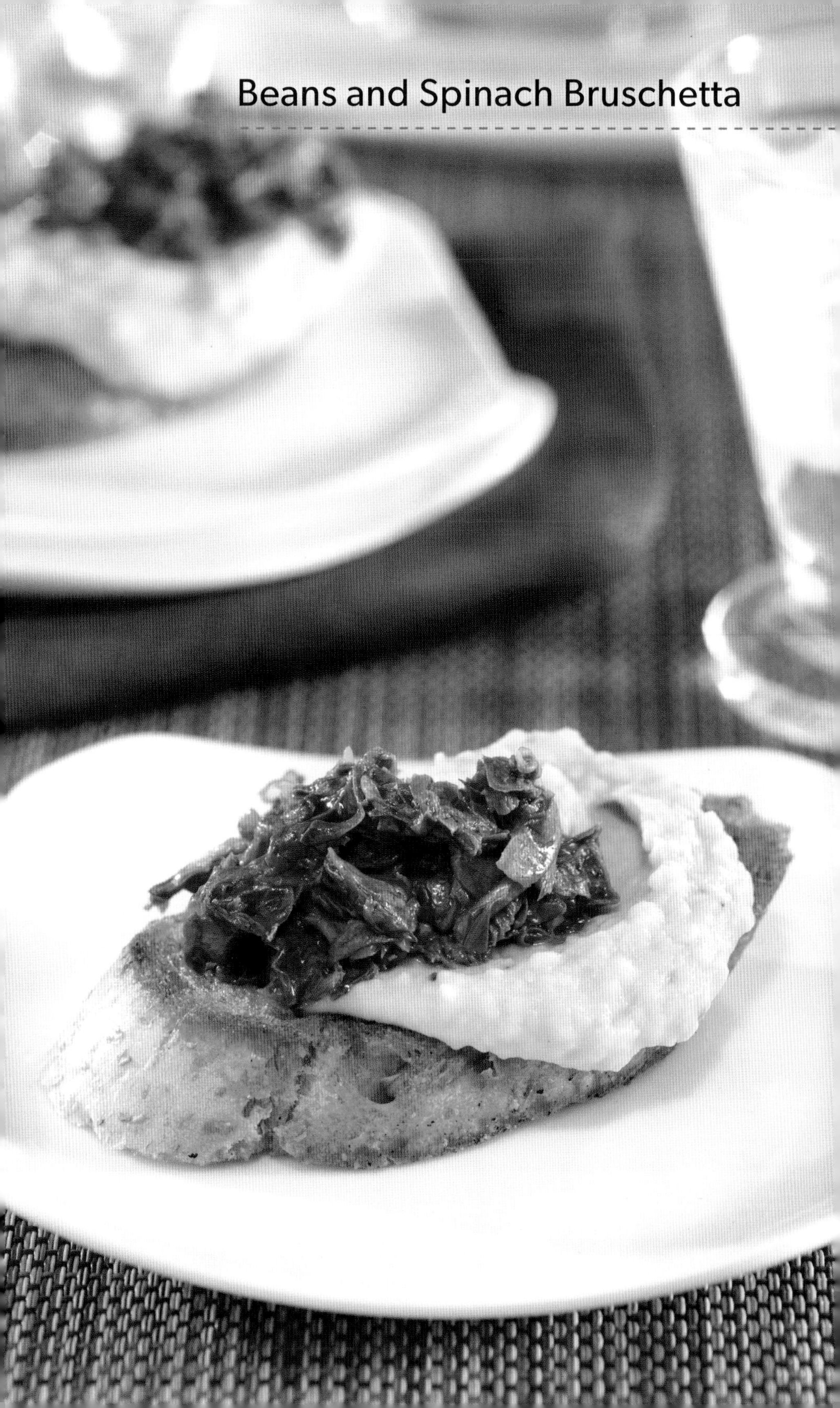

Mushroom Wild Rice

Makes 8 servings

1½ cups vegetable broth

1 cup uncooked wild rice

½ cup diced onion

½ cup sliced mushrooms

½ cup diced red or green bell pepper

1 tablespoon olive oil

Salt and black pepper

Combine broth, rice, onion, mushrooms, bell pepper, oil, salt and black pepper in **CROCK-POT®** slow cooker; stir to blend. Cover; cook on HIGH 2½ hours or until rice is tender and liquid is absorbed.

Potato Leek Soup

Makes 6 servings

1 container (32 ounces) vegetable broth

2 large baking potatoes (1½ to 2 pounds total), peeled and cubed

3 large leeks, white and light green parts thinly sliced (about 2 cups)

¼ teaspoon ground white pepper

½ cup sour cream

Chopped fresh chives or dill (optional)

1. Combine broth, potatoes, leeks and pepper in **CROCK-POT®** slow cooker; stir to blend. Cover; cook on LOW 7 to 8 hours or on HIGH 3 to 4 hours.

2. Purée soup in **CROCK-POT®** slow cooker using hand-held immersion blender. Or, remove mixture in batches to blender or food processor. Blend until smooth. (Soup can be refrigerated up to 2 days at this point.) Stir in sour cream. Sprinkle with chives just before serving, if desired.

Mushroom Wild Rice

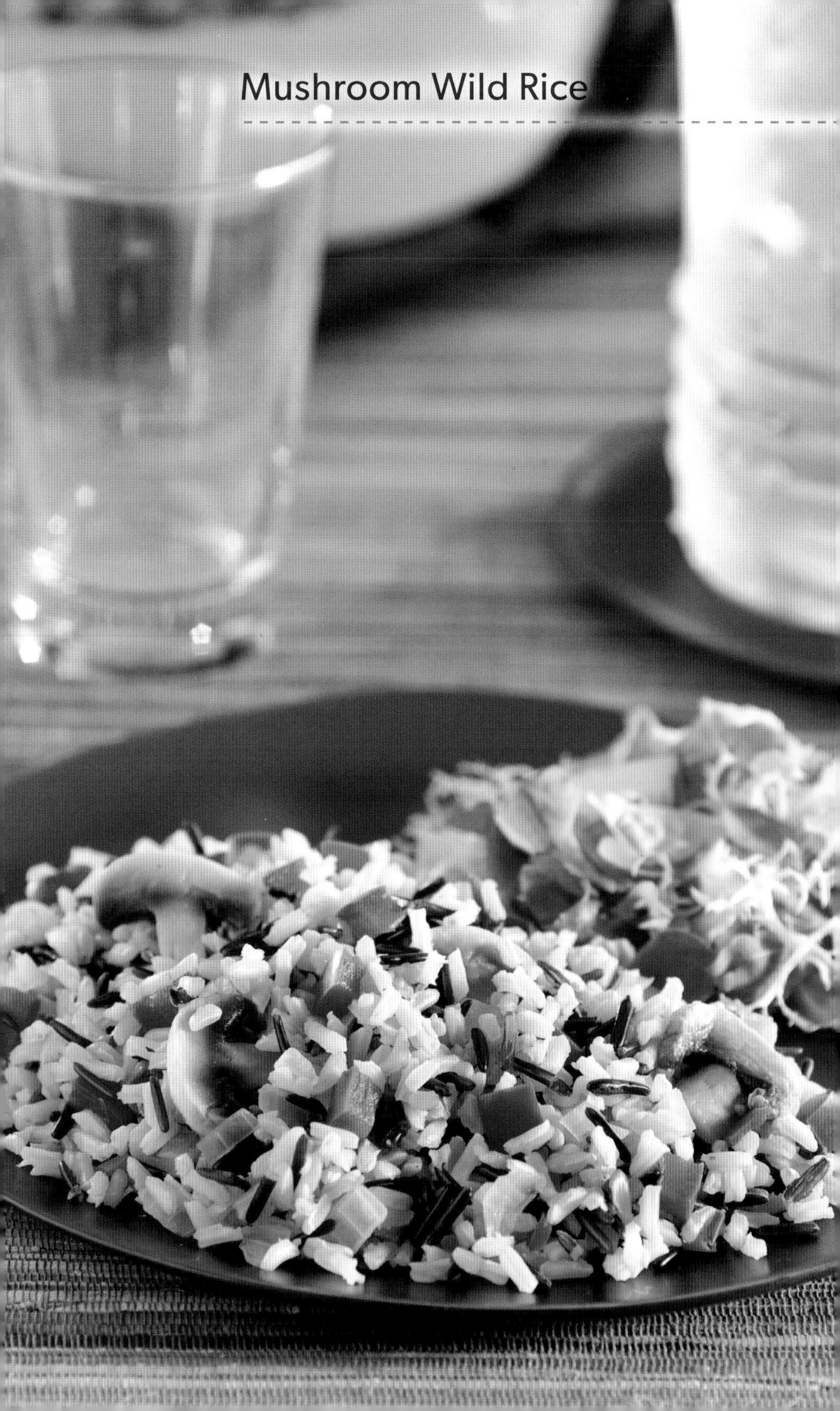

Orange-Spiced Glazed Carrots

Makes 6 servings

1 package (32 ounces) baby carrots

½ cup packed light brown sugar

½ cup orange juice

1 tablespoon butter

¾ teaspoon ground cinnamon

¼ teaspoon ground nutmeg

¼ cup cold water

2 tablespoons cornstarch

1. Combine carrots, brown sugar, orange juice, butter, cinnamon and nutmeg in **CROCK-POT®** slow cooker; stir to blend. Cover; cook on LOW 3½ to 4 hours. Remove carrots to large serving bowl using slotted spoon.

2. Turn **CROCK-POT®** slow cooker to HIGH. Stir water into cornstarch in small bowl until smooth; whisk into cooking liquid. Cover; cook on HIGH 15 minutes or until thickened. Spoon sauce over carrots.

Chili and Cheese "Baked" Potato Supper

Makes 4 servings

4 russet potatoes (about 2 pounds), unpeeled

2 cups prepared meatless chili

½ cup (2 ounces) shredded Cheddar cheese

¼ cup sour cream

2 green onions, sliced

1. Prick potatoes in several places with fork. Wrap potatoes in foil. Place in **CROCK-POT®** slow cooker. Cover; cook on LOW 8 to 10 hours or on HIGH 4 to 5 hours.

2. Carefully unwrap potatoes and place on serving dish. Place chili in medium microwavable dish; microwave at HIGH 3 to 5 minutes. Split potatoes and spoon chili on top. Sprinkle with cheese, sour cream and green onions.

Orange-Spiced
Glazed Carrots

Spinach Gorgonzola Corn Bread

Makes 1 loaf

2 boxes (8½ ounces *each*) corn bread mix

1 box (10 ounces) frozen chopped spinach, thawed and drained

1 cup crumbled Gorgonzola cheese

3 eggs

½ cup whipping cream

1 teaspoon black pepper

Paprika (optional)

1. Coat inside of 5-quart **CROCK-POT**® slow cooker with nonstick cooking spray. Combine corn bread mix, spinach, cheese, eggs, whipping cream, pepper and paprika, if desired, in medium bowl; stir to blend. Pour batter into **CROCK-POT**® slow cooker. Cover; cook on HIGH 1½ hours.

2. Turn off heat. Let bread cool completely before inverting onto large serving platter.

Note: Cook only on HIGH setting for proper crust and texture.

Cauliflower Mash

Makes 6 servings

2 heads cauliflower (8 cups florets)

1 tablespoon butter

1 tablespoon milk

Salt

Sprigs fresh Italian parsley (optional)

1. Arrange cauliflower in **CROCK-POT**® slow cooker. Add enough water to fill **CROCK-POT**® slow cooker by about 2 inches. Cover; cook on LOW 5 to 6 hours. Drain well.

2. Place cooked cauliflower in food processor or blender; process until almost smooth. Add butter; process until smooth. Add milk as needed to reach desired consistency. Season with salt. Garnish with parsley.

Spinach Gorgonzola Corn Bread

Cheesy Corn and Peppers

Makes 8 servings

2 pounds frozen corn

2 poblano peppers, chopped

2 tablespoons butter, cubed

1 teaspoon salt

½ teaspoon ground cumin

¼ teaspoon black pepper

3 ounces cream cheese, cubed

1 cup (4 ounces) shredded sharp Cheddar cheese

1. Coat inside of **CROCK-POT®** slow cooker with nonstick cooking spray. Combine corn, poblano peppers, butter, salt, cumin and black pepper in **CROCK-POT®** slow cooker. Cover; cook on HIGH 2 hours.

2. Stir in cheeses. Cover; cook on HIGH 15 minutes or until cheeses are melted.

Winter Squash and Apples

Makes 4 to 6 servings

1 teaspoon salt, plus additional for seasoning

½ teaspoon black pepper, plus additional for seasoning

1 butternut squash (about 2 pounds)

2 apples, sliced

1 medium onion, quartered and sliced

1½ tablespoons butter

1. Combine 1 teaspoon salt and ½ teaspoon pepper in small bowl.

2. Cut squash into 2-inch pieces; place in **CROCK-POT®** slow cooker. Add apples and onion. Sprinkle with salt and pepper mixture; stir well. Cover; cook on LOW 6 to 7 hours or until vegetables are tender.

3. Stir in butter and season to taste with additional salt and pepper.

Cheesy Corn and Peppers

Mashed Root Vegetables

Makes 6 servings

1 pound potatoes, peeled and cut into 1-inch pieces

1 pound turnips, peeled and cut into 1-inch pieces

12 ounces sweet potatoes, peeled and cut into 1-inch pieces

8 ounces parsnips, peeled and cut into ½-inch pieces

5 tablespoons butter

¼ cup water

2 teaspoons salt

¼ teaspoon black pepper

1 cup milk

1. Coat inside of **CROCK-POT®** slow cooker with nonstick cooking spray. Add potatoes, turnips, sweet potatoes, parsnips, butter, water, salt and pepper; stir to blend. Cover; cook on HIGH 3 to 4 hours.

2. Mash mixture with potato masher until smooth. Stir in milk. Cover; cook on HIGH 15 minutes.

Busy-Day Rice

Makes 4 servings

2 cups water

1 cup uncooked converted rice

2 tablespoons butter

1 tablespoon dried minced onion

1 tablespoon dried parsley flakes

2 teaspoons vegetable bouillon granules

Dash ground red pepper (optional)

Combine water, rice, butter, onion, parsley flakes, bouillon granules and ground red pepper, if desired, in **CROCK-POT®** slow cooker; stir to blend. Cover; cook on HIGH 2 hours.

Variation: During the last 30 minutes of cooking, add ½ cup green peas, broccoli florets or diced carrots.

Mashed Root Vegetables

Collard Greens

Makes 10 servings

4 bunches collard greens, stemmed, washed and torn into bite-size pieces

2 cups water

½ medium red bell pepper, cut into strips

⅓ medium green bell pepper, cut into strips

¼ cup olive oil

¼ teaspoon salt

¼ teaspoon black pepper

Combine collard greens, water, bell peppers, oil, salt and black pepper in **CROCK-POT®** slow cooker; stir to blend. Cover; cook on LOW 3 to 4 hours or on HIGH 2 hours.

Cheese Soup

Makes 4 servings

2 cans (10¾ ounces *each*) condensed cream of celery soup, undiluted

4 cups (16 ounces) shredded Cheddar cheese

1 teaspoon paprika, plus additional for garnish

1 teaspoon Worcestershire sauce

1¼ cups half-and-half

Salt and black pepper

Snipped fresh chives (optional)

1. Combine soup, cheese, 1 teaspoon paprika and Worcestershire sauce in **CROCK-POT®** slow cooker; stir to blend. Cover; cook on LOW 2 to 3 hours.

2. Add half-and-half; stir until blended. Cover; cook on LOW 20 minutes. Season to taste with salt and pepper. Sprinkle with additional paprika and chives.

Tip: Turn simple soup into a super supper by serving it in individual bread bowls. Cut a small slice from the tops of small, round loaves of a hearty bread (such as Italian or sourdough) and remove the insides, leaving a 1½-inch shell. Pour in soup and serve.

Collard Greens

Simmered Napa Cabbage with Dried Apricots

Makes 8 servings

4 cups napa cabbage or green cabbage, cored, cleaned and thinly sliced

1 cup chopped dried apricots

¼ cup clover honey

2 tablespoons orange juice

½ cup dry red wine

Salt and black pepper

Grated orange peel (optional)

1. Combine cabbage and apricots in **CROCK-POT**® slow cooker; toss to blend.

2. Combine honey and orange juice in small bowl; stir until smooth. Drizzle over cabbage. Add wine. Cover; cook on LOW 5 to 6 hours or on HIGH 2 to 3 hours.

3. Season with salt and pepper. Garnish with orange peel.

Rustic Cheddar Mashed Potatoes

Makes 8 servings

2 pounds russet potatoes, diced

1 cup water

2 tablespoons unsalted butter, cubed

¾ cup milk

¾ teaspoon salt

½ teaspoon black pepper

½ cup finely chopped green onions

2 tablespoons shredded Cheddar cheese

1. Combine potatoes, water and butter in **CROCK-POT**® slow cooker. Cover; cook on LOW 6 hours or on HIGH 3 hours. Remove potatoes to large bowl using slotted spoon.

2. Beat potatoes with electric mixer at medium speed 2 to 3 minutes or until well blended. Add milk, salt and pepper; beat 2 minutes or until well blended.

3. Stir in green onions and cheese. Turn off heat. Cover; let stand 15 minutes or until cheese is melted.

Simmered Napa Cabbage
with Dried Apricots

Slow-Good Apples and Carrots

Makes 6 servings

6 carrots, sliced into ½-inch slices

4 apples, peeled, cored and sliced

¼ cup plus 1 tablespoon all-purpose flour

1 tablespoon packed brown sugar

½ teaspoon ground nutmeg

1 tablespoon butter, cubed

½ cup orange juice

Layer carrots and apples in **CROCK-POT®** slow cooker. Combine flour, brown sugar and nutmeg in small bowl; sprinkle over carrots and apples. Dot with butter; pour in juice. Cover; cook on LOW 3½ to 4 hours.

Blue Cheese Potatoes

Makes 5 servings

2 pounds red potatoes, peeled and cut into ½-inch pieces

1¼ cups chopped green onions, divided

2 tablespoons olive oil, divided

1 teaspoon dried basil

½ teaspoon salt

¼ teaspoon black pepper

½ cup crumbled blue cheese

1. Layer potatoes, 1 cup green onions, 1 tablespoon oil, basil, salt and pepper in **CROCK-POT®** slow cooker. Cover; cook on LOW 7 hours or on HIGH 4 hours.

2. Gently stir in cheese and remaining 1 tablespoon oil. Cover; cook on HIGH 5 minutes. Remove potatoes to large serving platter; top with remaining ¼ cup green onions.

Slow-Good Apples
and Carrots

Chunky Ranch Potatoes

Makes 8 servings

3 pounds unpeeled red
potatoes, quartered

1 cup water

½ cup prepared ranch dressing

½ cup grated Parmesan or
Cheddar cheese

¼ cup minced fresh chives

1. Place potatoes in **CROCK-POT®** slow cooker. Add water. Cover; cook on LOW 7 to 9 hours or on HIGH 4 to 6 hours.

2. Stir in ranch dressing, cheese and chives. Break up potatoes into large pieces.

Beets in Spicy Mustard Sauce

Makes 4 servings

3 pounds beets, peeled, halved
and cut into ½-inch slices

¼ cup sour cream

2 tablespoons spicy brown
mustard

2 teaspoons lemon juice

2 cloves garlic, minced

¼ teaspoon black pepper

⅛ teaspoon dried thyme

1. Place beets in **CROCK-POT®** slow cooker. Add enough water to cover by 1 inch. Cover; cook on LOW 7 to 8 hours.

2. Combine sour cream, mustard, lemon juice, garlic, pepper and thyme in small bowl; stir to blend. Spoon over beets; toss to coat. Cover; cook on LOW 15 minutes.

Chunky Ranch Potatoes

French Onion Soup

Makes 8 servings

¼ cup (½ stick) butter

3 pounds yellow onions, sliced

1 tablespoon sugar

2 to 3 tablespoons dry white wine or water (optional)

8 cups vegetable broth

8 to 16 slices French bread (optional)

½ cup (2 ounces) shredded Gruyère or Swiss cheese

1. Melt butter in large skillet over medium-low heat. Add onions; cover and cook 10 minutes or just until onions are tender and transparent, but not browned.

2. Remove cover. Sprinkle sugar over onions; cook and stir 8 to 10 minutes or until onions are caramelized. Add onions and any browned bits to **CROCK-POT®** slow cooker. Add wine, if desired, to skillet. Bring to a boil, scraping up any browned bits. Add to **CROCK-POT®** slow cooker. Stir in broth. Cover; cook on LOW 8 hours or on HIGH 6 hours.

3. Preheat broiler. To serve, ladle soup into individual soup bowls. If desired, top each with 1 or 2 bread slices and about 1 tablespoon cheese. Place under broiler until cheese is melted and bubbly.

Variation: Substitute 1 cup dry white wine for 1 cup of vegetable broth.

Slow-Roasted Potatoes

Makes 8 servings

16 small new potatoes

3 tablespoons unsalted butter, cut into small pieces

1 teaspoon paprika

½ teaspoon salt

¼ teaspoon garlic powder

Black pepper

Combine potatoes, butter, paprika, salt, garlic powder and pepper in **CROCK-POT®** slow cooker; stir to blend. Cover; cook on LOW 7 hours or on HIGH 4 hours. Remove potatoes with slotted spoon to large serving dish. Add 1 to 2 tablespoons water to cooking liquid; stir until blended. Pour over potatoes.

French Onion Soup

Red Cabbage and Apples

Makes 6 servings

1 small head red cabbage, cored and thinly sliced

1 large apple, peeled and grated

¾ cup sugar

½ cup red wine vinegar

1 teaspoon ground cloves

Fresh apple slices (optional)

Combine cabbage, grated apple, sugar, vinegar and cloves in **CROCK-POT®** slow cooker; stir to blend. Cover; cook on HIGH 6 hours, stirring halfway through cooking time. Garnish with apple slices.

Coconut-Lime Sweet Potatoes with Walnuts

Makes 6 to 8 servings

2½ pounds sweet potatoes, cut into 1-inch pieces

8 ounces shredded carrots

¾ cup shredded coconut, toasted and divided*

¼ cup (½ stick) butter, melted

3 tablespoons sugar

½ teaspoon salt

¾ cup walnuts, toasted, coarsely chopped and divided**

2 teaspoons grated lime peel

To toast coconut, spread evenly on ungreased baking sheet. Toast in preheated 350°F oven 5 to 7 minutes or until light golden brown, stirring occasionally.

**To toast walnuts, spread in single layer in small heavy skillet. Cook and stir over medium heat 1 to 2 minutes or until lightly browned.*

1. Combine potatoes, carrots, ½ cup coconut, butter, sugar and salt in **CROCK-POT®** slow cooker. Cover; cook on LOW 5 to 6 hours. Remove to large bowl.

2. Mash potatoes with potato masher. Stir in 3 tablespoons walnuts and lime peel. Sprinkle with remaining walnuts and toasted coconut.

Red Cabbage and Apples

Mashed Rutabagas and Potatoes

Makes 8 servings

2 pounds rutabagas, peeled and cut into ½-inch pieces

1 pound potatoes, peeled and cut into ½-inch pieces

½ cup milk

½ teaspoon ground nutmeg

2 tablespoons chopped fresh Italian parsley

Sprigs fresh Italian parsley (optional)

1. Place rutabagas and potatoes in **CROCK-POT®** slow cooker; add enough water to cover vegetables. Cover; cook on LOW 6 hours or on HIGH 3 hours. Remove vegetables to large bowl using slotted spoon. Discard cooking liquid.

2. Mash vegetables with potato masher. Add milk, nutmeg and chopped parsley; stir until smooth. Garnish with parsley sprigs.

Spiced Sweet Potatoes

Makes 4 servings

2 pounds sweet potatoes, peeled and cut into ½-inch pieces

¼ cup packed dark brown sugar

1 teaspoon ground cinnamon

½ teaspoon ground nutmeg

⅛ teaspoon salt

2 tablespoons unsalted butter, cut into small pieces

1 teaspoon vanilla

Combine potatoes, brown sugar, cinnamon, nutmeg and salt in **CROCK-POT®** slow cooker; mix well. Cover; cook on LOW 7 hours or on HIGH 4 hours. Stir in butter and vanilla.

Mashed Rutabagas
and Potatoes

Metric Conversion Chart

VOLUME MEASUREMENTS (dry)

$^1/_8$ teaspoon = 0.5 mL
$^1/_4$ teaspoon = 1 mL
$^1/_2$ teaspoon = 2 mL
$^3/_4$ teaspoon = 4 mL
1 teaspoon = 5 mL
1 tablespoon = 15 mL
2 tablespoons = 30 mL
$^1/_4$ cup = 60 mL
$^1/_3$ cup = 75 mL
$^1/_2$ cup = 125 mL
$^2/_3$ cup = 150 mL
$^3/_4$ cup = 175 mL
1 cup = 250 mL
2 cups = 1 pint = 500 mL
3 cups = 750 mL
4 cups = 1 quart = 1 L

VOLUME MEASUREMENTS (fluid)

1 fluid ounce (2 tablespoons) = 30 mL
4 fluid ounces ($^1/_2$ cup) = 125 mL
8 fluid ounces (1 cup) = 250 mL
12 fluid ounces (1$^1/_2$ cups) = 375 mL
16 fluid ounces (2 cups) = 500 mL

WEIGHTS (mass)

$^1/_2$ ounce = 15 g
1 ounce = 30 g
3 ounces = 90 g
4 ounces = 120 g
8 ounces = 225 g
10 ounces = 285 g
12 ounces = 360 g
16 ounces = 1 pound = 450 g

DIMENSIONS

$^1/_{16}$ inch = 2 mm
$^1/_8$ inch = 3 mm
$^1/_4$ inch = 6 mm
$^1/_2$ inch = 1.5 cm
$^3/_4$ inch = 2 cm
1 inch = 2.5 cm

OVEN TEMPERATURES

250°F = 120°C
275°F = 140°C
300°F = 150°C
325°F = 160°C
350°F = 180°C
375°F = 190°C
400°F = 200°C
425°F = 220°C
450°F = 230°C

BAKING PAN SIZES

Utensil	Size in Inches/Quarts	Metric Volume	Size in Centimeters
Baking or Cake Pan (square or rectangular)	8×8×2	2 L	20×20×5
	9×9×2	2.5 L	23×23×5
	12×8×2	3 L	30×20×5
	13×9×2	3.5 L	33×23×5
Loaf Pan	8×4×3	1.5 L	20×10×7
	9×5×3	2 L	23×13×7
Round Layer Cake Pan	8×1½	1.2 L	20×4
	9×1½	1.5 L	23×4
Pie Plate	8×1¼	750 mL	20×3
	9×1¼	1 L	23×3
Baking Dish or Casserole	1 quart	1 L	—
	1½ quart	1.5 L	—
	2 quart	2 L	—